Writing Your Dissertation with Microsoft Word

A step-by-step guide

Vincent Kiernan

Published by Mattily Publishing, Alexandria, Virginia

www.mattily.com

Library of Congress Control Number: 2004117415

Publisher's Cataloging-in-Publication (Provided by Quality Books, Inc.)

Kiernan, Vincent.
Writing your dissertation with Microsoft Word / by Vincent Kiernan.
p. cm.
Includes index.

LCCN 2004117415
ISBN 0-9761868-0-2
ISBN 0-9761868-1-0 (PDF ed.)
ISBN 0-9761868-2-9 (LIT ed.)

1. Word processing. 2. Dissertations, Academic. 3. Microsoft Word. I. Title.
Z52.5.M52K53 2005   005.52
                    QBI05-200001

Printed in the United States of America

To Terri, Emily, and Matthew

CONTENTS

INTRODUCTION

Writing a thesis or dissertation is a Herculean effort. A graduate student must assimilate reams of information about the topic, conduct original research, and synthesize the new and existing research. In all this, word-processing software such as Word 2003 can make the graduate student's life much easier—or much more difficult. In most cases, long gone are the days when a graduate student employed a professional typist to prepare the thesis or dissertation manuscript. Today, most graduate students prepare their own manuscripts; relying on software makes it cheaper, quicker, and easier to make revisions.

But at the same time, many graduate students find it a daunting task to word process their own dissertations. Even if they have used the software previously for papers, creating a dissertation requires features of the software with which they are probably unfamiliar. When I was writing my own doctoral dissertation in 2001 and 2002, I was dismayed to find that manuals designed for general users often are confusing for graduate students, because they cover all of Word's features—whether or not they are useful in dissertations. Although the manuals describe Word's many options, they usually offer little guidance about *which* options a graduate student should choose when preparing a dissertation.

I hope that this manual will be much more useful to dissertation writers. I have consulted dissertation style manuals prepared by universities around the country to pinpoint the formatting issues that graduate students are most likely to encounter—and I give specific guidance on making the formatting choices.

I also hope that this manual will help graduate students do what they want to do—create new knowledge and complete their degrees—more quickly and easily.

How to use this book

This book is designed for a user who is familiar with Word at a basic level—someone who is able to create and open files, modify them, and save them. Many universities offer basic training courses in word-processing software, and if you are not able to perform such basic functions, you should consider taking such a course before you plunge into writing a dissertation with Word.

You need to gather two other resources before starting up Word: an up-to-date copy of your university's dissertation format rules and a copy of any other style manual you are planning to use, such as the *MLA Handbook for Writers of Research Papers* or the *Publication Manual of the American Psychological Association*. These will include style mandates that you must take into account frequently while working through this book, and you are well advised to keep copies close at hand throughout your work on the dissertation.

Note: The directions presented throughout this book will work with Word 2002 (also known as Word XP) as well as Word 2003. However, some of the directions will not work with versions of Word that are earlier than Word 2002.

Plan of the book

The book is structured as a how-to book rather than as a reference manual. That is, you work through the book from Chapter 1 to Chapter 8. (The exception is Chapter 9, which includes some general advice that you might want to read before starting.)

Chapter 1 helps you prepare a template for your dissertation. In Word 2003, a template is a blueprint that includes a wide variety of formatting information; documents that use the same template have the same formatting. Thus, by fashioning a template that meets your university's formatting rules at the very start, you ensure that all parts of your dissertation satisfy the rules and have a consistent look and feel. This saves you time as you write your dissertation and minimizes the possibility that your graduate school will require you to reformat the dissertation before it can be accepted.

Chapter 2 leads you through creating the various chapters for your dissertation. The following three chapters of this book show you how to add various special elements to those dissertation chapters: tables (Chapter 3), figures (Chapter 4), and equations (Chapter 5).

Chapter 6 helps you prepare the back matter of your dissertation—the appendices, bibliography, and the like. Chapter 7 demonstrates how to create the dissertation's preliminary pages—table of contents, list of tables, and so on. Chapter 8 shows you how to pull all the pieces of your dissertation into a single document that will wow your adviser and your other committee members.

CHAPTER 1

Creating a template for your dissertation or thesis

Templates are a powerful tool in Word 2003. A template can store a wide array of formatting information, including page setup characteristics such as margins and information about the fonts to be used in various parts of your dissertation. By using a single template as the basis for creating the various chapters and other parts of your dissertation, you can ensure that they all follow your institution's formatting rules. In addition, relying on a template makes it much easier to ensure that your dissertation follows a consistent style in those areas in which your university does leave you some latitude in formatting decisions.

Thus, it is a good investment of your time to fine-tune a template for your dissertation. In this chapter, we take a step-by-step approach to doing just that. Be sure to have a copy of your institution's dissertation style guide close at hand through this process so that you can be sure that the template meets the requirements of your institution.

The template that we configure in this chapter conforms to your institution's rules for chapters. Most institutions have somewhat different rules for the format of the front matter (title page, table of contents, etc.) and end matter (endnotes and/or references). We address these differing requirements in later chapters.

Some universities have already created Word templates that conform to their dissertation format rules. If so, use them, instead of following the directions in this chapter. (Microsoft itself offers a thesis template on its Web site. However, the template is not well configured for most dissertation requirements, and graduate students are well advised to avoid it and build their own templates from scratch.)

Note: It will be easiest for you to work through this chapter in one sitting. It may take an hour or two. However, should you need more than one session, the end of the chapter (sections 1.8 and 1.9) includes instructions on saving your template and then resuming editing it later.

To begin creating your dissertation template, launch Word 2003. The program will start and automatically create a blank document based on a built-in template called normal.dot. In the remainder of this chapter, we modify this template, rename it, and store it for future use as your dissertation template.

1.1   Page setup

Page Setup does what its name implies: It configures general characteristics of the pages in your document, including margins and page orientation. With your new file open, click **Page Setup** on the **File** menu. This brings up the **Page Setup** dialog box.

1.1.1   Margins

On the **Page Setup** dialog box, click on the **Margins** tab. In the **Top**, **Bottom**, **Left**, and **Right** boxes, fill in the margins for your dissertation, measured in inches. Most universities require dissertations to have a left margin of at least 1.5 inches, because the dissertation will be bound on the left-hand side. Rules for the top, right, and bottom margins vary by institution. As always, check your institution's dissertation style guide. (You can, but don't have to, use the inch symbol " after the numbers that you enter.)

Note: Some universities require larger top margins for the first page of every new major section, such as the start of a new chapter. We fine-tune the template for this requirement later (see section 1.4.1.2). For the moment, use the margin requirements for the second and additional pages of a chapter.

Leave **Gutter** at **0"** and **Gutter position** at **Left**. For **Orientation**, click on **Portrait,** which means that the long side of the page will lie along the vertical dimension. (Don't be concerned if you plan to have some landscape orientation pages in your dissertation—such as extra-wide tables—or special facing pages, which will be printed on the back of the page as bound in the dissertation. Chapter 2 shows you how to add these. For the moment, we are setting up your template for garden-variety pages in your dissertation.) In the **Pages** section, under **Multiple Pages**, be sure that **Normal** is selected; this instructs Word 2003 to use the same margins on all pages. In the **Preview** section, under **Apply to,** select **Whole Document**.

Example: The University of California at Berkeley mandates a left-hand margin of 1.5 inches and 1-inch margins on the three other sides. Figure 1-1 shows how to set these values.

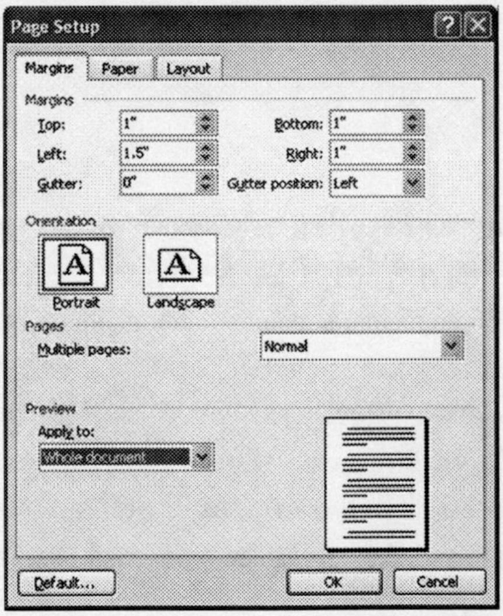

Figure 1-1

1.1.2 Paper

Next, click on the **Paper** tab. The defaults on this tab should not need to be changed, but double-check that the values are correct: **Paper size** should be set to **Letter, Width** should be **8.5"**, and **Height** should be **11"**. The settings for **Paper source** depend on the specific printer that you are using, but in general you probably want both **First**

page and **Other pages** set to the **Default** setting. Figure 1-2 shows the dialog box.

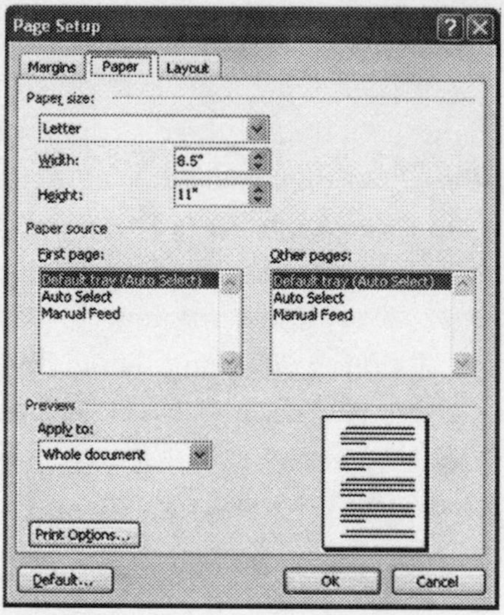

Figure 1-2

1.1.3   Layout

Next, click on the **Layout** tab. This box allows you to fine-tune the layout of your document. The **Section start** drop-down menu allows you to instruct Word 2003 on what to do when you instruct it to apply new formatting onward from a designated point in your file. From the options, select **Continuous.**

The **Header** and **Footer** sections of the **Layout** box allow you to control the placement of material that appears on every page, either between the text and the top of the page or between the text and the bottom of the page. Usually, the only item that appears in headers or footers of a dissertation is the page number. Consult your style guide to determine whether the page number should be in the bottom center, upper center, or the upper right—and exactly how far the page number should be from the top or bottom edge of the paper. Enter this value in the **Header** box (to have page numbers in the upper right or upper center) or **Footer** box (to have page numbers in the bottom center). (If your page numbers appear in the header, it is not a problem for there to be a number such as **0.5"** in the **Footer** box, or vice versa, because your footer will be blank anyway.) Make sure that **Different odd and even** is *not* checked.

A few universities require that the first page of a chapter have its page number in one spot on the page (perhaps the bottom center), while the other pages of the chapter have their page numbers in another location (perhaps the upper right). If this is the case for your institution, make sure that **Different first page** is checked. If your university has no such requirement, **Different first page** should *not* be checked.

Under **Page,** set **Vertical alignment** to **Top**; this pushes any extra white space to the bottom of your page, rather than centering the text in the middle of the page. Do not tinker with the **Line Numbers** and **Borders** boxes. These features are not used in dissertations.

Example: The University of Minnesota requires that page numbers be in the upper right-hand corner of the page, 1 inch from the top edge. Figure 1-3 shows how to configure the header.

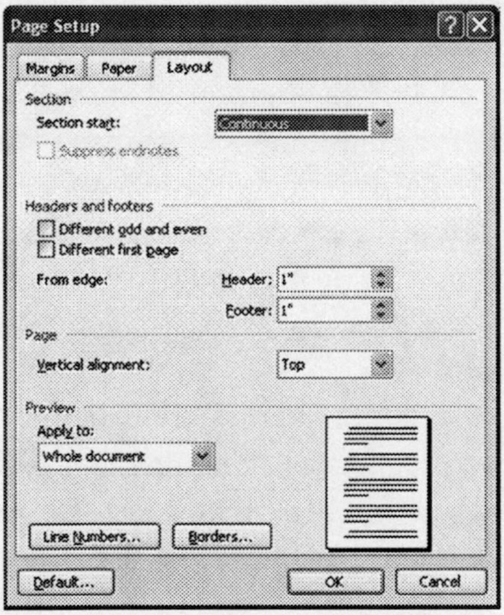

Figure 1-3

1.1.4 Updating the template

When you are done with all three tabs, click on the **OK** button in the bottom right-hand corner. The **Page Setup** box will vanish and the template will be updated.

1.2   Page numbers

Next, we finish configuring the template to handle page numbers correctly. As noted previously, most universities require page numbers to be in the bottom center, the top center, or the top right-hand corner of each page. In the previous step, we configured the template to correctly position the header or footer in which the page numbers will appear. In this step, we place the page number itself in the header or footer. (Some universities require that page numbers not appear on certain pages, such as the title page, or that they appear on the bottom center of pages that start chapters but the top right everywhere else. We will worry about these exceptions later. In this step, be sure to configure your template so that it correctly handles the page numbers for the second and additional pages of chapters.)

Under **Insert**, select **Page Numbers**. You will get the **Page Numbers** dialog box. From the **Position** drop-down menu, select whether the page numbers should be at the top of the page or the bottom of the page. From the **Alignment** drop-down menu, select whether you want page numbers to appear **Left, Center**, or **Right** on the page. (Ignore the **Inside** and **Outside** options.) Be sure **Show number on first page** is checked, unless your university requires that the first page of a chapter does not have a page number (few have this requirement).

Example: The University of Alaska at Fairbanks requires that page numbers appear in the top right of the page. Figure 1-4 shows how to accomplish this.

1.2.1   Page number format

Word 2003 can produce page numbers in a wide array of formats, but most universities require that the body of a dissertation—that is, the chapters and references and appendices—use Arabic numerals: 1, 2, 3, and so on. (Many universities also require that the front matter of the dissertation use lowercase Roman numerals: i, ii, iii, and so on. We make this adjustment later.)

To set the page number format for the body of your dissertation, click on the **Format** button in the **Page Number** dialog box. You will get the **Page Number Format** dialog box. Under the **Number format** drop-down menu, pick **1, 2, 3, …** , and under **Page numbering**, select the radio button for **Continue from previous section**. Click **OK** to get back to the **Page Setup** dialog box, and then **OK** again to leave **Page Setup**.

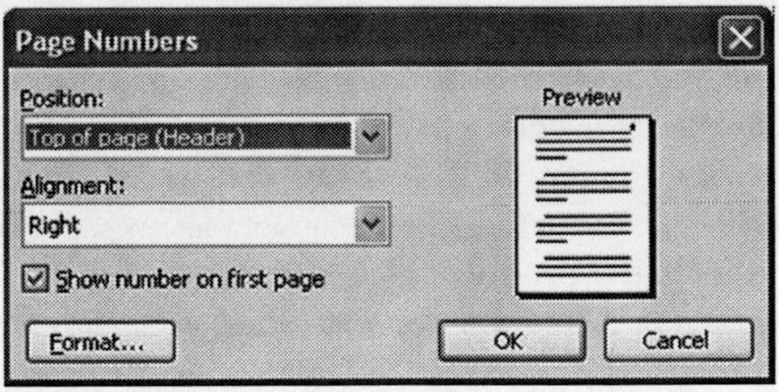

Figure 1-4

Example: The University of Delaware requires that the text pages and back matter in dissertations be numbered with Arabic numerals, from 1 to the last page. Figure 1-5 shows how to configure Word 2003 to meet this requirement.

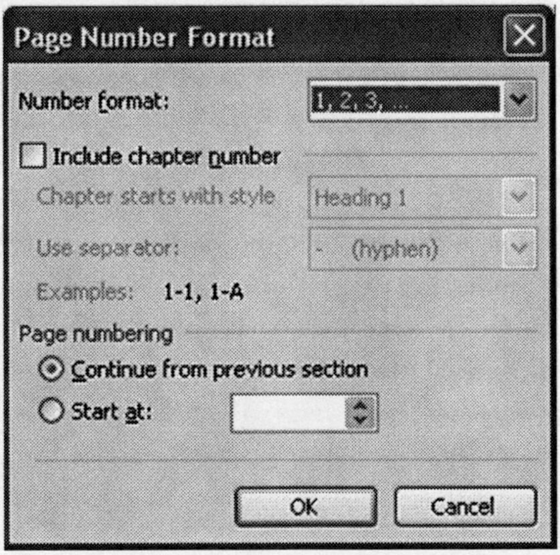

Figure 1-5

1.2.2   *Bottom center on the first page only*

Some universities require the first page of each chapter to have its page number in the bottom center but subsequent pages in the chapter to have numbers in the upper right. If you have followed the instructions in sections 1.1.3 and 1.2, you checked **Different first page** in the **Page Layout** dialog and you placed your page numbers in the upper right.

Now all you need to do is add the page number in the correct spot on the bottom of the first page. Place your cursor on the first page. Click on **View** and **Header and Footer** to get the **Header and Footer toolbar** and to see the header and footer for that page. Click once anywhere inside the dashed box labeled **First Page Footer**. Click on **Insert** and **Page Numbers** to get the **Page Numbers** dialog box (Figure 1-6). Set the **Alignment** drop-down menu to **Center**, and make sure that **Show number on first page** is *not* checked. Click **OK**. Click **Close** in the **Header and Footer toolbar.**

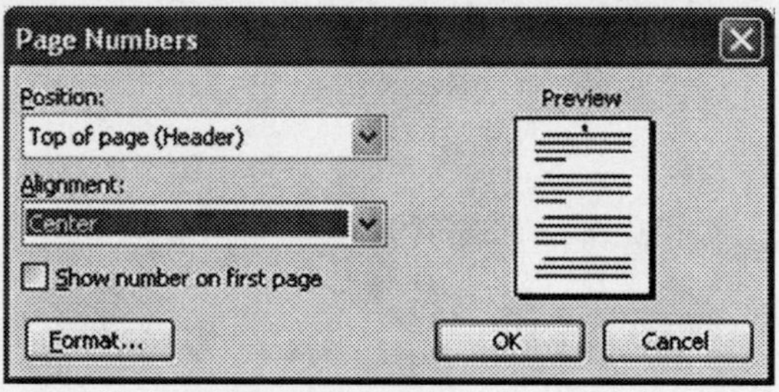

Figure 1-6

1.2.2.1 Adjusting centered page numbers

Some universities require that pages have unequal left and right margins but also require that page numbers be centered, either on the top or bottom of the page, between the physical edges of the page. This causes difficulties with Word 2003's automatic page number formatting, which centers numbers between margins rather than physical edges of a page. But it is possible to correct this problem.

First, follow the steps in the previous sections. Then click on **View** and then **Header and Footer** to get the **Header and Footer** toolbar. At the top and bottom of the page, you see a dashed area representing the header and footer for the page. The top or bottom box (depending on whether you selected the top or the bottom of the page for page numbers) contains the page number 1 (Figure 1-7). Click once directly on the number **1** and then click on **Format** and **Frame** (not **Frames**). In the **Frame** dialog box, in the **Horizontal** section, make sure the **Position** drop-down menu is set to **Center** and the **Relative to** drop-down menu is set to **Page** (Figure 1-8). Click **OK**, and the page number is moved to the physical center of the line, regardless of the positions of the left and right margins. Click **Close** in the **Header and Footer** toolbar.

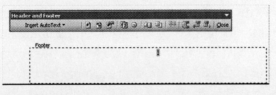

Figure 1-7

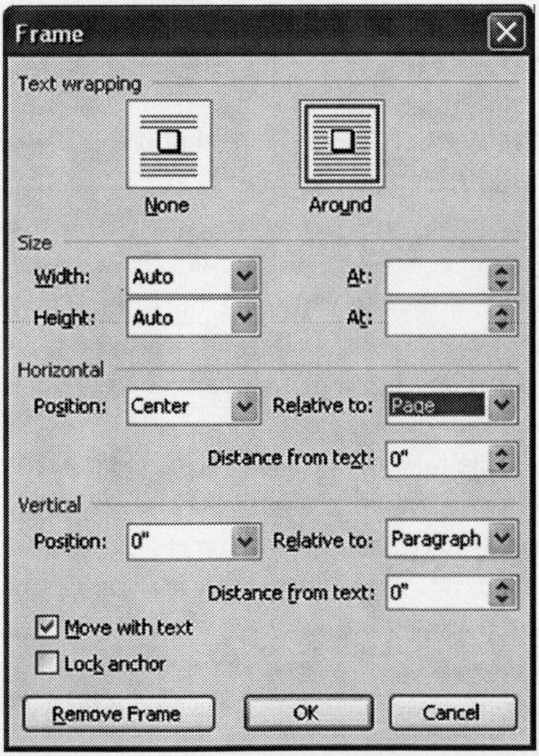

Figure 1-8

1.3   Default font

The font is the typeface used by Word 2003 to print your document and to display it on your monitor. Out of the box, Word 2003 comes equipped with a multitude of fonts, and Word 2003 can mix and match them (in any variety of sizes) to your heart's content. However, many graduate schools limit the style and size of fonts that can be used in a thesis or dissertation, so consult your style manual to determine what fonts are allowable in your dissertation.

In general, universities demand that the chapters, bibliography, and front matter of a dissertation all use the same font. However, some institutions do permit multiple fonts or font sizes, under limited conditions. For example, your university might allow one font in the text of the dissertation and another in the subheadings, or footnote fonts to be smaller than the body font and subheading fonts to be larger than the body font. Some institutions recommend that the body of the dissertation be produced in a *serif* font—a font such as Times and Times New Roman in which the ends of letters have small lines (serifs) projecting from them. These institutions also may recommend that headings be produced in a *sans serif* font—a font in which the letters have no serifs, such as Arial and Helvetica.

Font sizes are measured in a unit called points, in which 72 points equal 1 inch. Thus, all 12-point fonts are the same height (one-sixth of an inch). But all 12-point fonts are not necessarily the same width. For example, Courier characters are wider than Times New Roman characters, so a passage printed in 12-point Courier will take up more lines than the same passage printed in 12-point Times New Roman. If you are trying to reduce the number of pages in your dissertation without reducing the number of words, you may want to opt for Times New Roman for the body of your dissertation.

In Word 2003, a document template contains a "default font" setting—that is, the font characteristics that will be applied to a document unless you specifically override that setting, either in other styles in the template or by manually reformatting the document. Let's set the template's default font to the font that you wish to use for the body of your dissertation: On the **Format** menu, click **Font.** Select the font and size that you want. Ordinarily, you should pick the **Regular** font style, Underline style **(none)**, and font color **Automatic** (which generally produces black type); and you should make sure that all the special effects boxes are *not* checked. Then click the **Default** button. You get a dialog box asking you to verify the changes (Figure 1-9). Click **Yes** to accept.

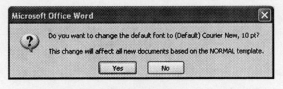

Figure 1-9

Tip: Resist the temptation to tweak the settings on the **Character Spacing** or **Text Effects** tabs for your default font. Modifying these settings almost certainly runs afoul of your graduate school's formatting rules.

Example: The University of Massachusetts at Amherst requires 10- or 12-point type. Allowable fonts include Courier, Helvetica, and Times Roman. Figure 1-10 shows how to configure the default font to be 10-point Courier.

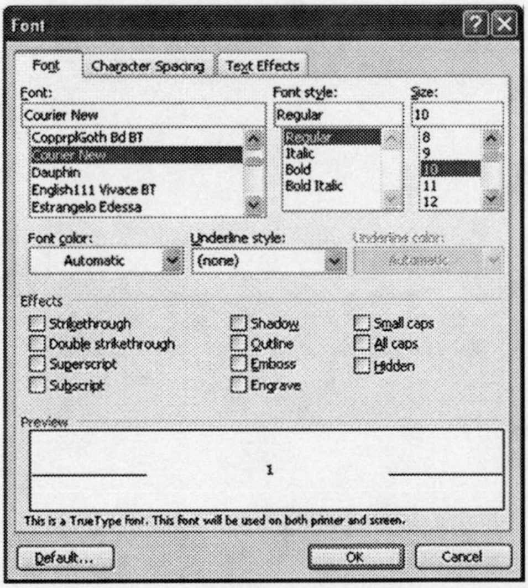

Figure 1-10

1.3.1　Line spacing

Many universities require that the body of a dissertation be double spaced; some permit line spacing of 1.5 lines. (Many also have special line spacing rules for footnotes, bibliography, or lengthy quotes. We deal with these later. Right now, we are setting the line spacing for the body of the dissertation.)

Under the **Format** menu, click on **Paragraph** and then on the **Indents and Spacing** tab. In the **Spacing** section, from the **Line spacing** pull-down menu select either **Double** (if you want double spacing) or **1.5 lines** (if you want 1.5-line spacing). Leave **At** blank and leave **Before** and **After** at **0 pt.** Click on **OK.**

Example: Michigan State University requires that the body of a dissertation be double spaced. The **Spacing** section in Figure 1-11 shows how to set that up.

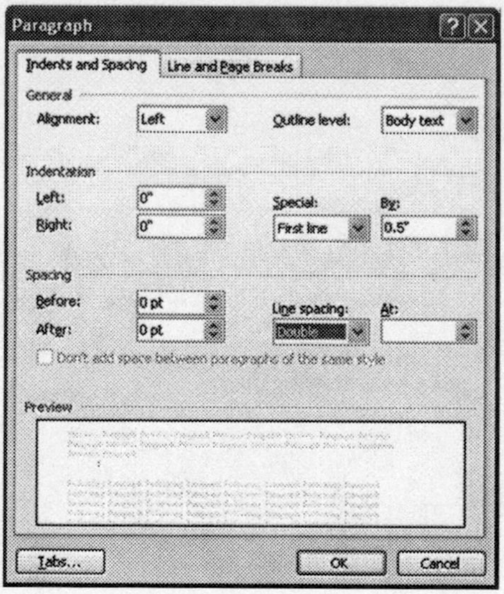

Figure 1-11

1.3.1.1   The "Exactly" setting

Although Word 2003 makes it quite easy to configure your document for single, 1.5, or double spacing, you may not be able to take advantage of this feature. If your dissertation includes superscripts or subscripts in a format other than Word's default, or if you must adjust the default size of your footnote or endnote numbers to comply with your university's formatting requirements (see sections 1.5.4 and 1.5.7), the default settings may create too much vertical space around any line that includes a superscript, subscript, footnote, or endnote. The result will be erratic line spacing in which some lines are correctly spaced and some are not.

Also, some universities do not allow the use of Word's automatic settings for 1.5-line or double spacing. The reason is that Word's settings are more generous than they should be for true 1.5-line or double spacing. That is, Word adds a little bit of additional white space, called leading (pronounced "ledding"), on top of each line of text. When figuring out how to do automatic line spacing, Word includes that extra leading. But some universities, by contrast, demand that dissertations be produced with "true" line spacing— that is, without the leading.

In either situation, you have to use Word 2003's "Exactly" line spacing feature, in which the user specifies the amount of space between lines and Word 2003 uses that amount of spacing, even if a line includes a superscript or subscript. If you use the **Exactly** feature in any portion of your dissertation, you should then use it throughout the entire dissertation, for consistent line spacing.

To use the **Exactly** capability, under the **Format** menu, click on **Paragraph** and then on the **Indents and Spacing** tab. In the **Spacing** section, from the **Line spacing** pull-down menu select

Exactly. If you are using 10-point type, set **At** to **15** for "true" 1.5-line spacing or **20** for double spacing. If you are using 12-point type, set **At** to **18** for 1.5-line spacing or **24** for double spacing. Leave **Before** and **After** at **0 pt**. Click on **OK.**

Example: Iowa State University requires the use of **Exactly** line spacing. Suppose you were formatting your document in 12-point type and wanted to use double spacing. The **Spacing** section of Figure 1-12 shows how to configure Word 2003 in this manner.

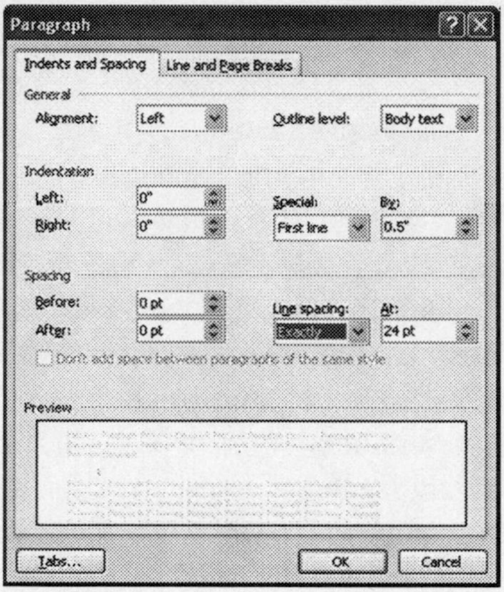

Figure 1-12

1.3.1.2 Indentation

Most universities want each new paragraph in a dissertation to start with an indent, rather than having the text flush left and skipping a line between paragraphs. This is how you set the indentation:

Under the **Format** menu, click on **Paragraph** and then on the **Indents and Spacing** tab. In the **Indentation** section, from the **Special** pull-down menu, select **First line**. In the **By** box, type the amount of indentation that you want, in inches. (Half an inch, or **0.5"**, generally works well and comports with most dissertation formatting rules.) Click **OK**.

Example: The University of Miami requires that each paragraph be indented. Figure 1-13 shows how to add a 0.5" indentation at the start of each paragraph.

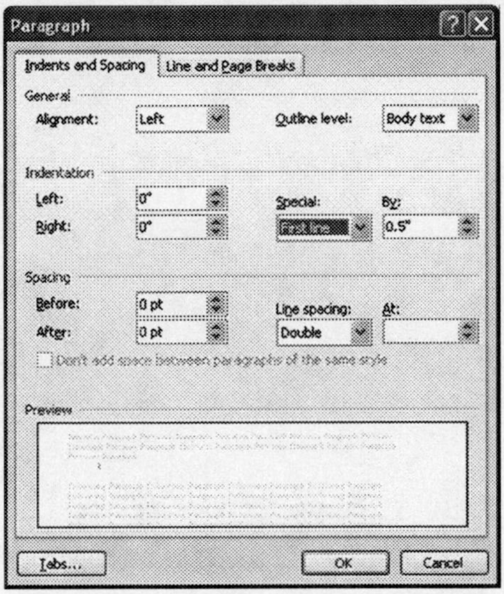

Figure 1-13

By contrast, some universities permit each paragraph to start flush left, with white space added between each paragraph. Although you could simply hit the **Return** key twice after each paragraph, you can configure your template to add the extra white space automatically. Under the **Format** menu, click on **Paragraph** and then on the **Indents and Spacing** tab. In the **Indentation** section, from the **Special** pull-down menu, select **(none)**. In the **Spacing** section, leave **Before** at **0** but set **After** to twice the point size that you are using in your body text. That is, if you are using

10-point type, set **After** to **20**; if you are using 12-point type, set **After** to **24**. Click on **OK**.

Example: The University of Central Florida allows paragraphs to be separated by white space if the start of the paragraphs is not indented. Figure 1-14 shows how to configure Word 2003 to format paragraphs in this fashion.

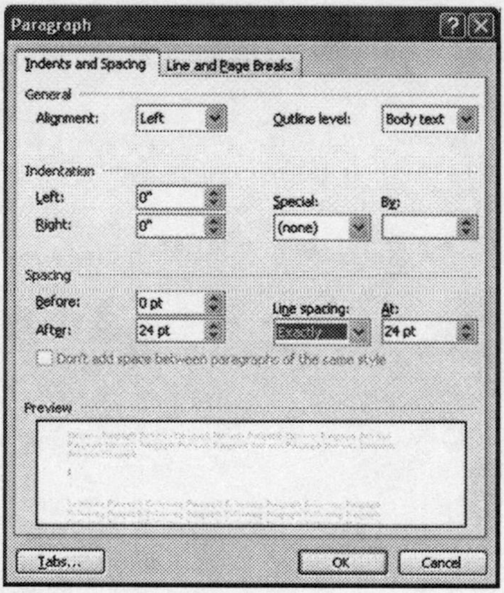

Figure 1-14

1.3.1.3 Alignment

Most universities call for the text of the dissertation to be left aligned (also known as left justified); that is, the left edges of each line of printing are aligned along the left margin, but the right edges of text are "ragged." To have your text left aligned, click on the **Format** menu, next on **Paragraph,** and then on the **Indents and Spacing** tab. Pick **Left** from the **Alignment** drop-down menu in the **General** section of the **Indents and Spacing** tab.

Example: Howard University discourages the use of full justification and instead recommends left justification. Figure 1-15 shows how to make this setting.

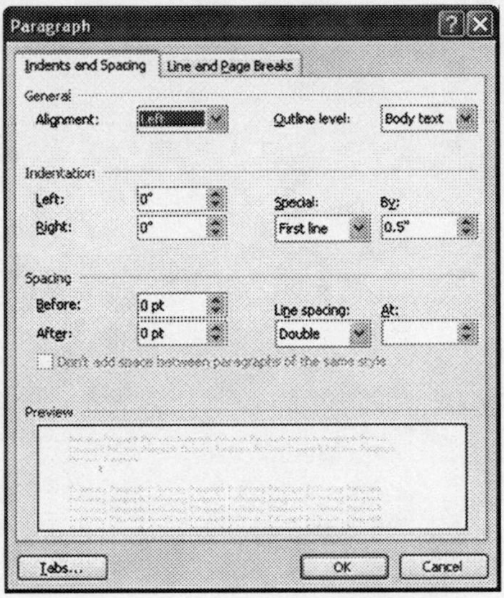

Figure 1-15

Some universities do permit dissertations to be fully justified rather than left aligned. In this format, which is used in most books and newspapers, the left and right edges of each line of printing extends to the left and right margins of the page. To create this effect, Word 2003 inserts extra spacing between words and letters. To create fully justified text, pick **Justified** from the **Alignment** drop-down menu. Click **OK**. (Also, for the sake of consistency, be sure to do the same thing when creating your styles for block quotations, footnotes, endnotes, and your bibliography; see sections 1.5.1, 1.5.2, 1.5.5, and 1.5.8.)

Example: The University of Georgia allows fully justified text. Figure 1-16 shows how to configure Word 2003 to produce justified text.

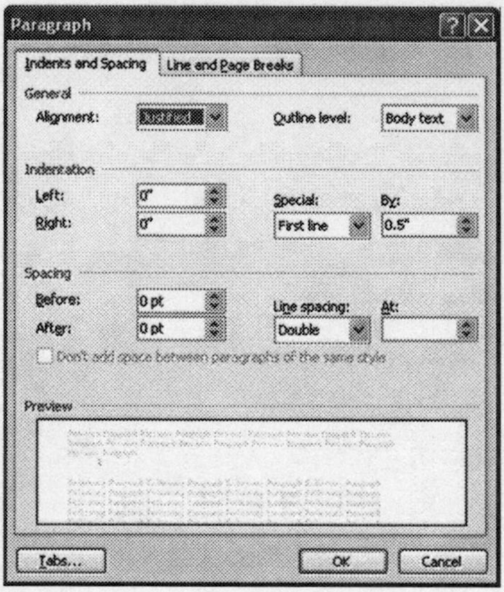

Figure 1-16

1.3.1.4   Widows and orphans

When a paragraph starts at the end of one page and is continued on a second page, with only the first line of that paragraph remaining on the first page, that first line is often called a widow. Similarly, if only the last line of the paragraph appears on the second page, that last line is called an orphan. Word 2003 can automatically eliminate widows and orphans by putting the page break before or after the paragraph in question. Some graduate schools encourage the use of this option. To add this to your template, do this:

Under the **Format** menu, click on **Paragraph**, and then on the **Line and Page Breaks** tab. Check the **Widow/Orphan control** box. Click **OK**.

Example: Cornell University forbids orphans and discourages widows. Figure 1-17 shows how to configure Word 2003 to suppress both.

Note: Fully suppressing widows and orphans also requires an additional step in configuring the formatting of headings and sub-headings (see section 1.4.2.3).

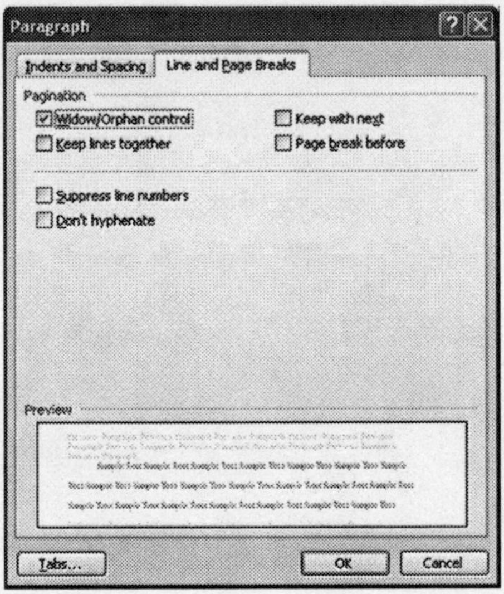

Figure 1-17

1.4   Creating formats for titles and headings

Dissertations generally are divided into several chapters, and each chapter may be further divided by headings and even subheadings within each heading. Although you can type these chapter titles and headings as regular text, that approach would fail to take advantage of Word 2003's capability to build a table of contents from your headings—if you encode the headings correctly. In this section, we configure your chapter titles and headings so that they conform to your university's formatting rules and so that Word 2003 will be able to use them to create a table of contents for your document. In most cases, we revise Word 2003's built-in styles, although we may create one heading style from scratch.

First, let's configure Word 2003 to give you information on all the styles that are available on your computer. Click on **Format** and then on **Styles and Formatting**. This opens a pane on the right side of your screen, titled **Styles and Formatting**. Select **Custom…** from the **Show** drop-down menu. The **Format Settings** dialog box comes up (Figure 1-18). In this dialog box, set the **Category** drop-down menu to **All styles** and click the **Show all** button. Then click **OK** to close the **Format Settings** box.

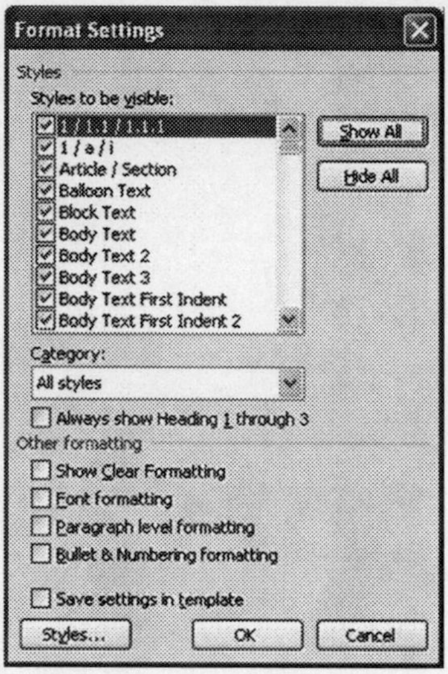

Figure 1-18

1.4.1   Chapter title

Each dissertation chapter, or other major division, starts with a title. We next adapt Word 2003's style named Heading 1 for such titles. Click on **Format** and then on the **Styles and Formatting** pane. The section titled **Pick formatting to apply** lists available styles; scroll through this list until you find **Heading 1**.

Right-click on it with your mouse and select **Modify** from the shortcut menu that appears. The **Modify Style** dialog box appears, listing **Heading 1** as the style's name (Figure 1-19). In the **Properties** section, under **Style based on**, pick **Normal** from the pull-down menu, and for **Style for following paragraph**, pick **Normal** from the pull-down menu. Be sure the **Automatically update** box is *not* checked. Do *not* click **OK** quite yet.

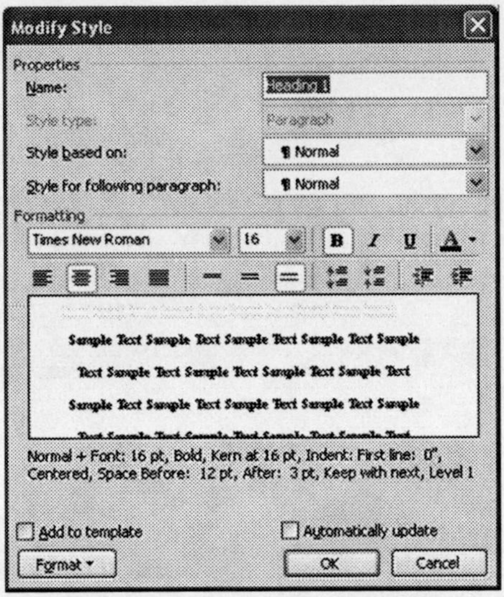

Figure 1-19

1.4.1.1 Fonts

To set the typeface characteristics for your chapter title, on the **Modify Style** page, click the **Format** button and then click the **Font** button to bring up the **Font** dialog box. Here, select the font characteristics of your chapter title. It is usually acceptable for the chapter title to be of the same font and size as your body text. But some universities permit a larger point size, bold face, or even a different font. Check your university's requirements to be sure.

Some style manuals also have rules about the casing of chapter titles. That is, a university may require that the chapter title be all uppercase or upper and lowercase. If your chapter title is supposed to be in all uppercase, do **not** type it that way in the text; rather, be sure that under **Effects**, the **All caps** box is checked. Or if your chapter title is supposed to be underlined, select the single-line icon from the **Underline style** drop-down menu. If the title is supposed to be boldface or italicized, select **Bold** or **Italic** from the **Font style** selections. Following this protocol will ensure that the chapter title appears properly formatted in the body of the text but in plain text in the table of contents. Most universities prefer this approach.

Click **OK** when you're done setting your font requirements, to return to the **Modify Style** page. Do not click **OK** on the **Modify Style** page yet.

Example: Iowa State University allows chapter titles to be in a different font from the body text and as much as 4 points larger than the body text. Figure 1-20 shows how to configure Word 2003 to create chapter titles in 16-point Times New Roman.

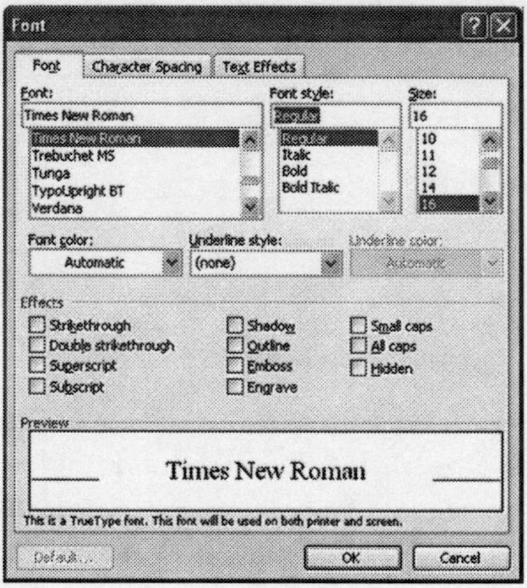

Figure 1-20

Example: American University requires chapter titles to be printed in capital (uppercase) letters and not underlined. Figure 1-21 shows how to make those settings, assuming that you were going to use 12-point Times New Roman.

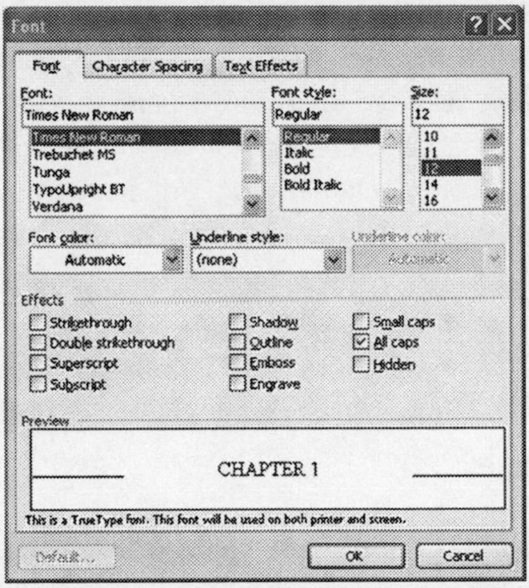

Figure 1-21

1.4.1.2   Indents and spacing

The next step is to configure your chapter title so it appears in the correct location on the page. Consult your style manual: Is the major heading supposed to be centered? Or perhaps flush left? Also, some universities require that the first page of a new chapter have a deeper margin at the top of the page than the top margins for the rest of the body text. Check your style manual on this point as well.

To set these characteristics, on the **Modify Style** page, click on the **Format** button, then on **Paragraph**, and finally on the **Indents and Spacing** tab. In the **General** section, from the **Alignment** drop-down menu, select the style in which your heading is supposed to appear: **Centered**, if in the middle of the line; **Left**, if flush left. From the **Outline level** drop-down menu, make sure that **Level 1** is selected. This will ensure that the chapter titles are reproduced correctly if you open your document in **Outline** view, and it will help in producing the table of contents.

In the **Indentation** section, make sure that **Left** and **Right** are both set to **0"** and that the **Special** drop-down menu is set to **(none)**.

Under **Spacing**, set **Before** to **0 pt** unless your university requires an extra-generous top margin for the first page of a chapter. If it does require a larger top margin, here is how to figure out the value for **Before**: Take your university's required top margin (in inches) for the chapter start, and subtract the value of the standard top margin that your university requires other pages to have (again, in inches). The remainder is the amount of space, in inches, that your style has to include before the chapter title; multiply this number by 72 to convert it into points. Enter this number in the **Before** field.

If you want a single blank line between your chapter title and the text that follows, set **After** to the point size of your body font (i.e., **10 pt** if you are using a 10-point font and **12 pt** if you are using a 12-point font). If you want 1.5 lines of space after the title, set **After** to **15 pt** if you are using 10-point type and **18 pt** if you are using 12-point type.

Line spacing comes into play if you have a heading that is so long that it exceeds one line of text. In such a situation, the value for **line spacing** determines the spacing between those lines. Pick a value from the drop-down menu that is consistent with your institution's rules. Many universities require that multiple lines of a single heading be single spaced; if that's the case at your institution, select **Single** from the drop-down menu. (But if you are using Word's **Exactly** setting elsewhere in your document [section 1.3.1.1], select **Exactly** from the drop-down menu and set **At** to **10 pt** for single-spaced 10-point type or **12 pt** for single-spaced 12-point type.)

Click **OK** to close the **Paragraph** dialog box and bring you back to the **Modify Style** page. Do not click **OK** on the **Modify Style** page yet.

Example: The University of Massachusetts at Lowell requires a 1-inch top margin in its dissertations—except for the first page of a new chapter, which must begin 2 inches from the top edge of the page. To calculate the value for **Before**, subtract the 1-inch standard margin from the 2-inch margin for a chapter start, and conclude that the chapter title style must create an additional 1 inch, or 72 points, of top margin before the chapter title. Figure 1-22 shows how to configure Word 2003 for this requirement.

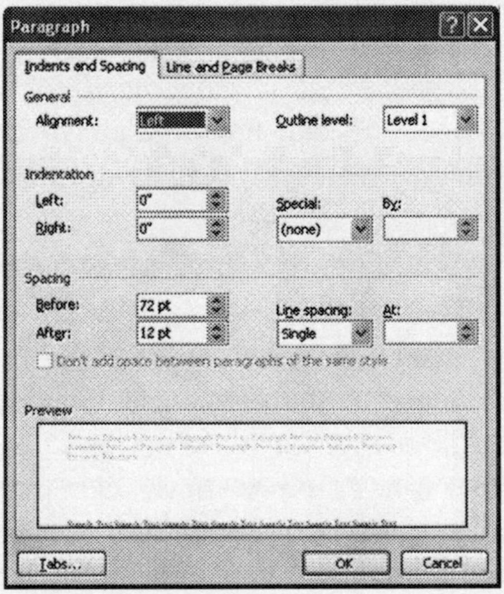

Figure 1-22

1.4.1.3   Numbered headings

Word 2003 can number the headings in your dissertation in a way that represents the structure of your dissertation; some institutions permit this. For example, the major sections of Chapter 1 could be numbered 1.1, 1.2, 1.3, and so forth, while the subdivisions of Section 1.1 could be numbered 1.1.1, 1.1.2, 1.1.3, and so forth. However, if you want to use numbered headings, check carefully regarding the style of the numbering scheme that is allowed. Word 2003 offers many possibilities, and you want to pick one that your institution permits.

To select a numbered style for your chapter titles, click the **Format** button on the **Modify Style** page, then the **Numbering** menu option, and then on the **Outline Numbered** tab. Click once on the numbering style that you wish to use in your headings. If you wish, you can click on the **Customize** button and adjust settings such as the style of numerals and the tab settings used in the numbering. (**Customize** will be grayed out unless one of the numbered styles is selected.) Click **OK** in the **Outline Numbered** tab to finish setting up your numbering. Do not click **OK** to close the **Modify Style** dialog box.

1.4.1.4   Keyboard shortcut

You can save yourself formatting time by assigning a keyboard shortcut to the style for your chapter titles. Whenever you press the specified combination of keys, the text at the cursor will be formatted according to the designated style.

To create a shortcut, click the **Format** button on the **Modify Style** page and then the **Shortcut key** menu option. The **Customize Keyboard** dialog box comes up.

Press your desired combination of keys simultaneously; the combination must include at least one of the **Alt, Ctrl,** or **Shift** keys. They will be displayed in the **Press new shortcut key** box; if they are already assigned as a shortcut, a message reports that. If they are available for use as a shortcut, Word 2003 reports that they are currently assigned to [**unassigned**]. (Figure 1-23 shows the example of setting the combination of the **Alt** and **V** keys as a shortcut for the Heading 1 style.) If you wish to assign this as a shortcut for this style, click the **Assign** key. Using the **Save changes in** drop-down menu, you can decide whether you want this keyboard shortcut to be available whenever you use Word 2003 (if so, select **normal.dot**). Or if you want this keyboard shortcut to be available only when you are using the dissertation template or documents based on it, select the name of your template file from the drop-down menu. If you haven't saved the file yet, its name will probably be Document1 or something similar; if you previously did save the template file (see section 1.8), it will be named **My Dissertation.dot**. In any case, the file's name is listed in the top left of your computer screen, to the left of the phrase "Microsoft Word."

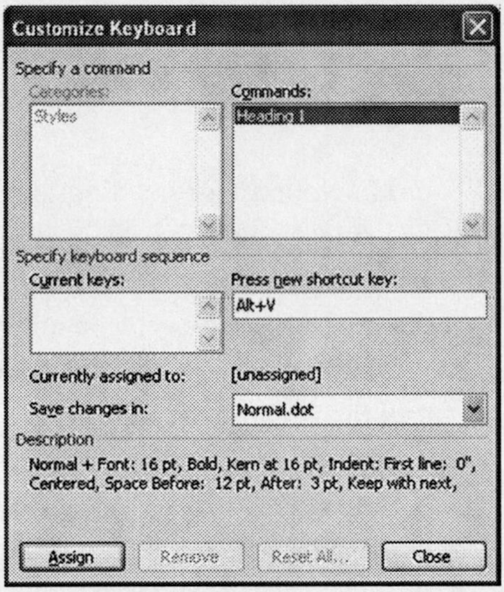

Figure 1-23

When you are done assigning shortcuts, click **Close** to bring you back to the **Modify Style** page.

1.4.1.5 Finishing up

When you are done configuring Heading 1, click **OK** on the **Modify Style** page to save your settings.

1.4.2 Major headings

Each dissertation chapter usually is divided into sections, each of which begins with a major heading. Dissertation style manuals use a variety of terms for this type of division; some may refer to this as a first-level heading, and others may call it a major division. Formatting these is similar in most respects to formatting the chapter title: We revise existing styles in Word 2003.

Open **Format** and then the **Styles and Formatting** task pane. In the **Pick formatting to apply** section, scroll through the list until you find **Heading 2**. Right-click on it with your mouse and select **Modify** from the shortcut menu that appears. The **Modify Style** dialog box appears, listing **Heading 2** as the style's name. For **Style based on**, pick **Normal** from the pull-down menu, and for **Style for following paragraph**, pick

Normal from the pull-down menu. Be sure the **Automatically update** box is *not* checked. Do not click on **OK** yet.

1.4.2.1   Fonts

First, set the font for your major headings. On the **Modify Style** page, click on the **Format** button and then on **Font**. On the **Font** page, select the font characteristics that meet your university's requirements. If the major heading is to be all uppercase, be sure that the **All caps** box is checked here. If your major headings must be underlined, select the single-line icon from the **Underline style** drop-down menu. If major headings are supposed to be boldface or italicized, select **Bold** or **Italic** from the **Effects** selections. Click **OK** when you're done setting your font requirements, to return to the **Modify Style** page. Don't click on **OK** yet.

1.4.2.2   Indents and spacing

Then configure your major heading so that it appears in the correct location on the page, whether flush left or centered. On the **Modify Style** page, click on the **Format** button, then on **Paragraph**, and finally on the **Indents and Spacing** tab. In the **General** section, from the **Alignment** drop-down menu select the location for your heading: **Centered**, if in the middle of the line, and **Left**, if flush left. In the **Indentation** section, make sure that **Left** and **Right** are both set to **0"** and that the **Special** drop-down menu is set to **(none)**.

From the **Outline level** drop-down menu, pick **Level 2**. This will ensure that the major headings are displayed correctly if you open your document in Outline view, and it will help in producing the table of contents.

Under **Spacing**, set **Before** to **0 pt** (unless your university requires extra spacing between the end of one major section and the start of another; if so, enter that requirement, in points). For **After**, if you want a single blank line between your major heading and the text that follows, enter the point size of your body font, that is, **10 pt** if you're using a 10-point font and **12 pt** if you're using a 12-point font. If you want 1.5 lines of space after the heading, set **After** to **15 pt** if you're using 10-point type and **18 pt** if you're using 12-point type.

Line spacing comes into play if you have a heading that is so long that it exceeds one line of text. In such a situation, the value for **Line spacing** determines the spacing between those lines. Pick a value from the drop-down menu that is consistent with your institution's rules. Many universities require that multiple lines of a single heading be single-spaced. If that's the case at your institution, select **Single** from the drop-down menu. (But if you're using Word's **Exactly** setting [section 1.3.1.1], select **Exactly** from the drop-down menu and set **At** to **10 pt** for single-spaced 10-point type or **12 pt** for single-spaced 12-point type.)

When done, click on **OK** to close the **Paragraph** page and bring you back to **Modify Style**. Do not click on **OK** yet.

1.4.2.3   Widows and orphans

If you previously configured Word 2003 to suppress widows and orphans in your body text (see section 1.3.1.4), you should also configure your major headings to suppress them as well.

On the **Modify Style** page, click on the **Format** button, then on **Paragraph**, and finally on the **Line and Page Breaks** tab. Be sure that the **Widow/orphan control** and **Keep with next** boxes are checked; the first box prevents widows and orphans, and the second box prevents a page break coming between the major heading and the first line of the paragraph that follows it. Click on **OK** to close the **Paragraph** page and bring you back to **Modify Style**.

Example: Princeton University discourages headings and sub-headings appearing on the last line of a page. Figure 1-24 shows how to configure Word 2003 to make sure that headings and sub-headings are not on the last line of a page.

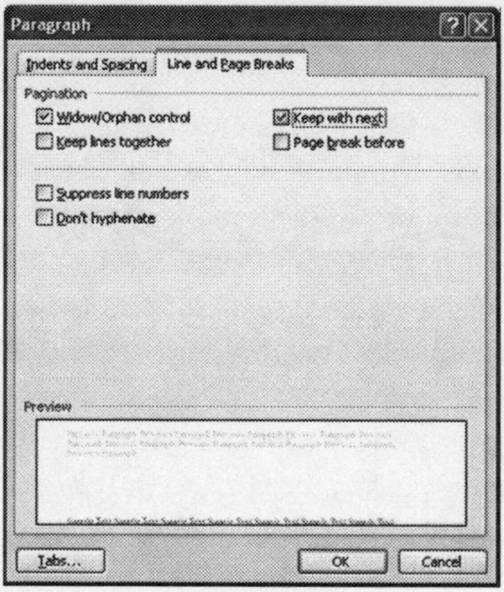

Figure 1-24

1.4.2.4   Numbered headings

As with chapter titles, you can instruct Word 2003 to number your major headings (see section 1.4.1.3). Although Word 2003 allows some heading levels to be numbered even if other headings are unnumbered, your university may want all your headings to be in one format or the other.

To select a numbered style for your major headings, click the **Format** button on the **Modify Style** page, then the **Numbering** menu option, and then on the **Outline Numbered** tab. Click once on the numbering style that you wish to use in your headings. If you wish, you can click on the **Customize** button and adjust settings such as the style of numerals and the tab settings used in the numbering. Click **OK** in the **Outline Numbered** tab to finish setting up your numbering.

1.4.2.5   Keyboard shortcut

Consider setting a keyboard shortcut for your major heading style. Follow the same steps as described in section 1.4.1.4.

1.4.2.6   Finishing up

When you are done configuring the format for major headings, click **OK** in the **Modify Style** dialog box.

1.4.3   Minor headings

Each subdivision of a chapter can be further divided into minor headings. Creating the style for these headings is very similar to the previous steps for revising existing heading styles to accommodate chapter titles and major headings. Click on **Format,** then open the **Styles and Formatting** task pane. In the **Pick formatting to apply** section, scroll through the list until you find **Heading 3**. Right-click on it with your mouse and select **Modify** from the shortcut menu that appears. The **Modify Style** dialog box appears, listing **Heading 3** as the style's name. For **Style based on**, pick **Normal** from the pull-down menu, and for **Style for following paragraph**, pick **Normal** from the pull-down menu. Be sure the **Automatically update** box is *not* checked.

1.4.3.1   Fonts

To set the font for your minor headings, on the **Modify Style** page, click on the **Format** button and then on **Font**. On this page, select the font characteristics that meet your university's requirements. As with the previous headings, be sure to check the **All caps** box if the minor headings are to be rendered in all upper-case, select the single-line icon from the **Underline style** drop-down menu if the minor headings are to be underlined, or select **Bold** or **Italic** from the Effects menu if the minor headings are to be in bold face or italicized. Click **OK** when you're done setting your font requirements, to return to the **Modify Style** page. Do not click **OK** yet.

1.4.3.2   Indents and spacing

Then configure your minor heading so that it appears in the correct location on the page, whether flush left or centered. On the **Modify Style** page, click on the **Format** button, then on **Paragraph**, and finally on the **Indents and Spacing** tab. In the **General** section, from the **Alignment** drop-down menu select the location for your minor heading: **Centered**, if in the middle of the line, and **Left**, if flush left. In the **Indentation** section, make sure that **Left** and **Right** are both set to **0"**. The **Special** drop-down menu is set to **(none)** unless the minor headings are to be indented the same way that paragraphs are. If this is the case, select **First line** from the **Special** drop-down menu and set **By** to the same amount of indentation that you used in section 1.3.1.2.

From the **Outline level** drop-down menu, pick **Level 3**. This will ensure that the minor headings are displayed correctly in **Outline** view, and it will help in producing the table of contents.

Under **Spacing**, set **Before** to **0 pt**. For **After**, if you want a single blank line between your minor headings and the text that follows, enter the point size of your body font, that is, **10 pt** if you're using a 10-point font and **12 pt** if you're using a 12-point font. If you want 1.5 lines of space after the heading, use **15 pt** if you're using 10-point type and **18 pt** if you're using 12-point type.

Line spacing comes into play if you have a heading that is so long that it exceeds one line of text. In such a situation, the value for **Line spacing** will determine the spacing between those lines. Pick a value from the drop-down menu that is consistent with your institution's rules. Many universities require that multiple lines of a single heading be single spaced. If that's the case at your institution, select **Single** from the drop-down menu. (But if you're using Word's **Exactly** setting, select **Exactly** from the drop-down menu and set **At** to **10 pt** for single-spaced 10-point type or **12 pt** for single-spaced 12-point type.)

When done, click on **OK** to close the **Paragraph** page to bring you back to the **Modify Style** page, but do not yet click **OK** on the **Modify Style** page.

1.4.3.3   Widows and orphans

If you previously configured Word 2003 to suppress widows and orphans in your body text (see section 1.3.1.4), you should also configure your minor headings to suppress them as well.

On the **Modify Style** page, click on the **Format** button, then on **Paragraph**, and finally on the **Line and Page Breaks** tab. Be sure that the **Widow/orphan control** and **Keep with next** boxes are checked. The first box prevents widows and orphans, and the second box prevents a page break coming between the major heading and the first line of the paragraph that follows it. Click on **OK** to close the **Paragraph** page and bring you back to **Modify Style**. Do not click **OK** yet on the **Modify Style** page.

1.4.3.4   Numbered headings

As with chapter titles and major headings, you can instruct Word 2003 to number your minor headings (see section 1.4.1.3). To select a numbered style for your minor headings, click the **Format** button on the **Modify Style** page, then the **Numbering** menu option, and then the **Outline Numbered** tab. Click once on the numbering style that you wish to use in your headings. If you wish, click on the **Customize** button and adjust settings such as the style of numerals and the tab settings used in the numbering. (**Customize** will be grayed out unless one of the numbering styles is selected.) Click **OK** in the **Outline Numbered** tab to finish setting up your numbering.

1.4.3.5   Keyboard shortcut

Consider setting a keyboard shortcut for your minor heading style. Follow the same steps as described in section 1.4.1.4.

1.4.3.6   Finishing up

When you're done configuring the format for minor headings, click **OK** in the **Modify Style** dialog box.

1.4.4   Further subheadings

You may find a need for further subdivisions of your dissertation. Word 2003 can accommodate up to nine levels of headings. But as a practical matter (and sometimes due to university rules), you probably want to limit yourself to two or three levels.

To create the format for deeper subdivisions, follow the same steps as described for minor headings in section 1.4.3. For each level, modify a heading style with a number that is 1 greater than the previous heading (i.e., you would modify Heading 4, then Heading 5, etc.). Set the formatting to correspond to your university's requirements for each level of subheadings. Increase the value of the **Outline level** by 1 for each new level of subheadings. If you numbered your other headings, you should consider numbering the new subdivisions as well (section 1.4.1.3). Consider creating a keyboard shortcut for each subheading (see section 1.4.1.4).

1.4.5   Headings for preliminary pages

You must also create a style for the titles of your preliminary pages that you do not want listed in the table of contents—such as the dedication page, the acknowledgments page, and the contents page. It should be identical to your Heading 1 style, except that it should be configured to be excluded from the table of contents.

Click **Format**, then the **Styles and Formatting** task pane. Click on the **New Style** button to bring up the **New Style** dialog box. In the **Name** field, enter **Preliminary page**. From the **Style type** drop-down menu, select **Paragraph**. For **Style based on**, pick **Heading 1** from the pull-down menu, and for **Style for following paragraph**, pick **Normal** from the pull-down menu. Be sure the **Automatically update** box is *not* checked.

On the **New Style** page, click the **Format** button and then click the **Font** button to bring up the **Font** dialog box. Here, select font characteristics identical to those that you selected for Heading 1 (section 1.4.1.1). Click **OK** when you're done setting your font requirements, to return to the **New Style** page.

Then, on the **New Style** page, click on the **Format** button, then on **Paragraph**, and finally on the **Indents and Spacing** tab. In the **General, Indentation,** and **Spacing** sections, choose values identical to those you used for Heading 1 (section 1.4.1.2). From the **Outline level** drop-down menu, make sure that **Body Text** is selected. Click **OK** to close the **Paragraph** dialog box and bring you back to the **New Style** page. Click **OK** again to close the **New Style** page.

1.5   Creating styles for your body text

When you configured the default font (section 1.3), you already set the characteristics for most of your body text. However, you still need to create styles for other parts of your text. In what follows, you can skip any section that applies to formatting that you won't use; for example, if you're not going to use footnotes in your dissertation, you can skip the sections on creating styles for footnotes, footnote separators, and footnote numbers.

1.5.1   Block quotations

Many dissertations contain lengthy quotations. Most style manuals require that short quotations be printed within quotation marks, as regular text, but that longer quotations—known as block quotations—be set off from the other text, with different margins and/or line spacing.

Definitions of block quotations vary. For example, Turabian's *A Manual for Writers of Term Papers, Theses, and Dissertations* defines a block quotation as a quotation of two or more sentences that takes eight or more lines, and the American Psychological Association's style manual defines a block quotation as a quotation of 40 or more words. Universities often have their own definitions.

We next create a style called **Block Quotations** that you can use with block quotations (however your institution or style manual defines a block quotation). Click on **Format** and then **Styles and Formatting**. Click on the **New Style** button.

In the **New Style** dialog box, enter the name **Block Quotation** in the **Name** field. For **Style type**, pick **Paragraph** from the pull-down menu. For **Style based on**, pick **Normal** from the pull-down menu, and for **Style for following paragraph**, pick **Normal** from the pull-down menu. (Figure 1-25 shows what the dialog box looks like.)

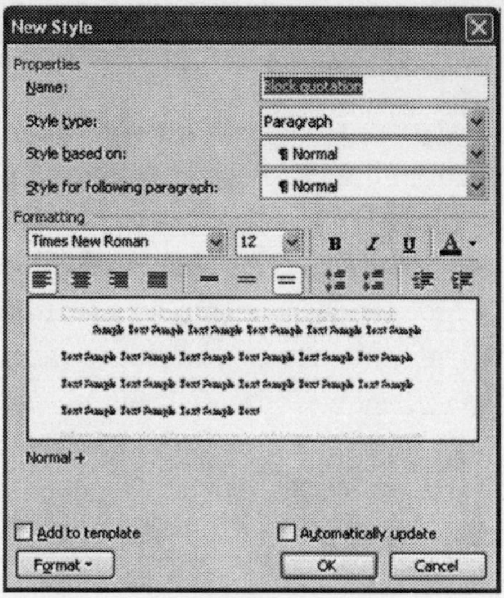

Figure 1-25

To set the margins and line spacing for your block quotations, click the **Format** button in the lower left hand of the dialog box and click on **Paragraph**. In the **Paragraph** dialog box, click on the **Indents and Spacing** tab.

In the **General** section under **Alignment,** pick **Left** from the drop-down menu, unless your dissertation uses fully justified text (section 1.3.1.3), in which case you should select **Justified**. In the **Indentation** section, set **Left** and **Right** to the left and right indentations for your block quotations, as directed by your dissertation style manual. The first line of block quotations usually does not have a paragraph indentation, so under **Special**, pick **(none)** from the drop-down menu.

In the **Spacing** section of the dialog box, set **Before** to **0 pt,** unless your dissertation style manual demands extra line spaces before or after a block quotation. Set **After** to the point size of the type that you are using for your body text, that is, set it to **10 pt** if you are using 10-point type or **12 pt** if you are using 12-point type. This will create an extra line between the quotation and the paragraph that follows it. From the **Line spacing** drop-down menu, select the required line spacing for the inside of the block quotation (for most universities, this will be **Single**), unless you're using Word's **Exactly** setting (section 1.3.1.1). Leave **At** blank. Click **OK**.

Example: New Mexico State University requires that block quotations be single spaced, with the left-hand margin indented 0.5 inch and with no additional indentation of the right-hand margin. Figure 1-26 shows how to set these parameters.

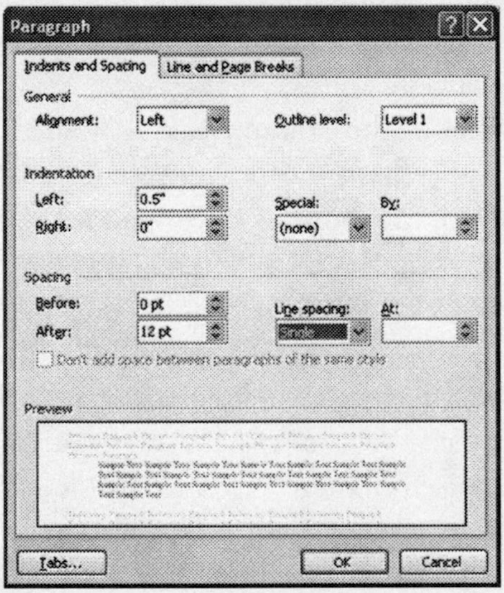

Figure 1-26

Clicking **OK** on the **Paragraph** dialog box returns you to the **New Style** dialog box. While here, you may wish to create a keyboard shortcut for this style (see section 1.4.1.4). When you're done creating the shortcut, or if you choose not to create one, click **OK** in the **New Style** dialog box, and your Block Quotation style will be ready for you to use.

1.5.2   Footnotes

Footnotes appear at the bottom of the page, optionally set off from the main text by a separator mark. They can be used to document sources or for a brief digression from the text. Not all style manuals permit footnotes.

Word 2003 comes with a built-in style for footnotes, which you can modify to suit the requirements of your dissertation format rules. Click on **Format** and then on **Styles and Formatting.** In the **Styles and Formatting** pane, be sure that the **Show** drop-down menu is set to **All Styles**. Under **Pick formatting to apply,** look for an entry for **Footnote Text.** (If there is no listing for **Footnote Text,** set **Show** to **Custom...** to open the **Format Settings** dialog box. Under **Styles to be visible**, click in the box in front of **Footnote Text** so that a check mark appears in the box. Set the **Category** drop-down menu to **All styles** and click on **OK** to close the **Format Settings** dialog box.)

Then right-click on the **Footnote Text** style and then select **Modify**. First set the typeface characteristics for your footnotes. On the **Modify Style** page, click on the **Format** button and then on **Font**. On this page, set the font characteristics for your footnotes. Most universities permit footnotes to be the same font and point size as body text, so these are usually safe choices. Some universities do permit footnotes to be in a smaller point size than the body text. As always, check your style manual to be sure. Click **OK** when you are done with the font characteristics, which will return you to the **Modify Style** dialog box. Do not click **OK** yet in the **Modify Style** dialog box.

Example: Michigan State University allows 10-point fonts for footnotes. Figure 1-27 shows how to configure footnotes to use 10-point Arial.

Then set the line spacing for your footnotes. Some universities demand that footnotes be double-spaced; others permit single spacing. Click the **Format** button in the lower left of the **Modify Style** dialog box and click on **Paragraph**. In the **Paragraph** dialog box, click on the **Indents and Spacing** tab.

In the **General** section, under **Alignment**, pick **Left** from the drop-down menu, unless your dissertation uses fully justified text (section 1.3.1.3), in which case you should select **Justified**.

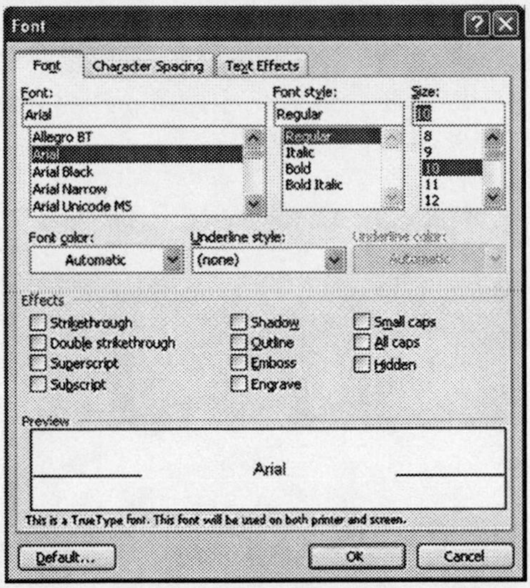

Figure 1-27

In the **Indentation** section, set **Left** and **Right** to **0"**. Under **Special**, pick **(none)** from the drop-down menu if you do not want the first line of the footnote text indented. If you do want the first line indented, pick **First line** and set **By** to the amount of indentation you want (generally **0.5"** works well). If you want the second and subsequent lines of every footnote item to be indented, select **Hanging** and set **By** to the desired amount of indentation (again, **0.5"** works well).

In the **Spacing** section of the dialog box, set **Before** to **0 pt**. Set **After** to **0 pt** if you don't want any blank space between footnotes. If you want a single line of space between each footnote, enter the point size of your body font (i.e., **10 pt** if you're using a 10-point font and **12 pt** if you're using a 12-point font). If you want 1.5 lines of space between footnotes, use **15 pt** if you're using 10-point type and **18 pt** if you're using 12-point type.

From the **Line spacing** drop-down menu, select the required line spacing for footnotes (typically, either **Double** or **Single**). Leave **At** blank. (But if you're using Word's **Exactly** setting, select **Exactly** from the drop-down menu and set **At** to **10 pt** for single-spaced 10-point type, **15 pt** for 10-point type with 1.5-line spacing, **20 pt** for double-spaced 10-point type, **12 pt** for single-spaced 12-point type, **18 pt** for 12-point type with 1.5-line spacing, and **24 pt** for double-spaced

12-point type.) Click **OK** on the **Paragraph** dialog box, which will return you to the **Modify Style** dialog box.

Example: Portland State University allows footnotes to be single spaced. Figure 1-28 shows how to set up single-spaced footnotes.

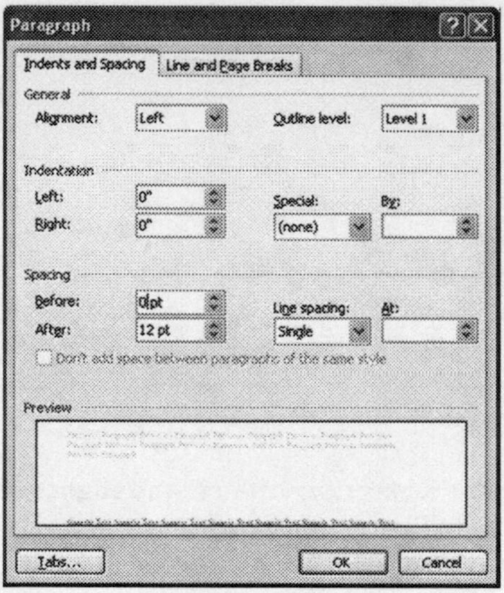

Figure 1-28

You may wish to create a keyboard shortcut for this style (see section 1.4.1.4). When you're done, or if you choose not to create a shortcut, click **OK** in the **Modify Style** dialog box, and your footnote style will be ready for you to use.

1.5.3   *Footnote separators*

Word 2003 provides three elements for separating footnotes from the regular text on the page:

1. The *footnote separator,* which Word inserts between the body text and the first line of footnotes on the page. The default value is a 2-inch unindented line.

2. The *footnote continuation separator,* which is used when a footnote is continued from one page to another. The footnote continuation separator is inserted between the body text and the first line of the continuation of the footnotes on the next page. The default value is a line from the left margin to the right margin.

3. The *footnote continuation notice,* which is also used when a foot-note is continued from one page to another. The notice is placed after the last line of the part of the footnote that fits on the first page. The default value is to have no continuation notice.

These settings are consistent with many style manuals, but you can change them. To do so, however, you must have inserted at least one footnote into your document. To insert the footnote, put your cursor anywhere in the body of your template document. Click on **View** and then on **Normal** to select Word's so-called **Normal** viewing mode. Click on **Insert**, then **Reference**, and then **Footnote**. The **Footnote and Endnote** dialog box comes up (Figure 1-29). Under **Location**, click **Footnotes** and then click **Insert**. The **Footnotes** pane opens at the bottom of the page (Figure 1-30). From the **Footnotes** drop-down menu, select **Footnote Separator** or **Footnote Continuation Separator** or **Footnote Continuation Notice**, depending on which you want to modify (Figure 1-31 shows the footnote separator). The desired separator appears in the **Footnotes** pane. Modify it, or delete it, as you wish. Click on another separator if you wish to do more modifications, or click **Close** when you're done. Finally, be sure to delete the footnote number in your text at this stage; the footnote will be deleted, but the changes to the separators or continuation notice will be retained.

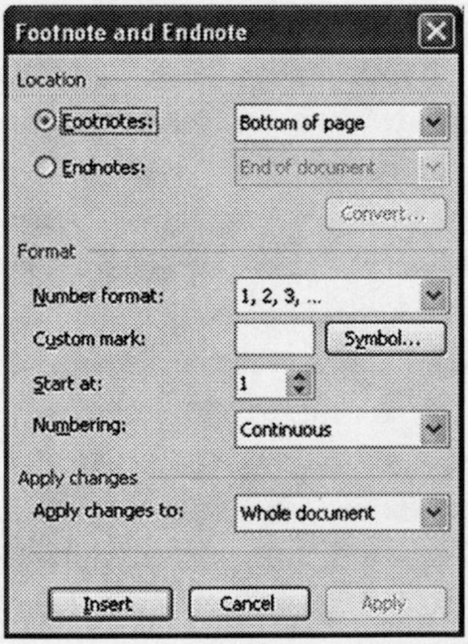

Figure 1-29

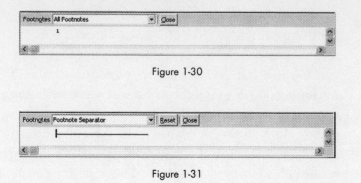

Figure 1-30

Figure 1-31

1.5.4   Footnote numbers

To produce the small superscript numbers used in footnotes, Word 2003 by default uses the same font as the body text—but in a smaller point size. For example, footnote numbers for text printed in 12-point Times New Roman would be generated in 8-point Times New Roman. This is acceptable at some institutions. Others, however, require that footnote numbers be larger than the default so that they will be large enough to be readable in microfilmed copies of the dissertation.

To change the type size of your footnote numbers, click on **Format** and then on **Styles and Formatting.** In the **Styles and Formatting** pane, be sure that the **Show** drop-down menu is set to **All Styles**. Under **Pick formatting to apply,** look for an entry for **Footnote Reference.** (If there is no listing for **Footnote Reference,** set **Show** to **Custom...** to open the **Format Settings** dialog box. Under **Styles to be visible**, click in the box in front of **Footnote Reference** so that a check mark appears in the box. Set the **Category** drop-down menu to **All styles** and click on **OK** to close the **Format Settings** dialog box.)

Then right-click on the **Footnote Reference** style and then select **Modify.** On the **Modify Style** page, click on the **Format** button and then on **Font**. Make sure the **Font** box lists the same font that you are using in the body of your dissertation and that **Font style** is set to **Regular.** In the **Font size** box, pick the font size that you want your footnote numbers to have. Under **Effects**, be sure that the **Superscript** box is *not* checked. Then click on the **Character Spacing** tab. From the **Position** drop-down menu, pick **Raised**; in the **By** field, enter the number of points that you would like the number to be above the text.

(A reasonable value to try is half the point size of your body type, that is, 5 if you are using 10-point type and 6 if you are using 12-point type.) Click **OK** to get back to the **Modify Style** page. Be sure the **Automatically update** box is *not* checked, and then click **OK** again.

Caution: If you modify the size of your footnote numbers, you must also set the line spacing to **Exactly.** Otherwise, Word 2003 produces erratically spaced lines in your dissertation. See section 1.3.1.1.

Example: Figure 1-32 illustrates how to set the character spacing to elevate the position of the footnote number by 5 points.

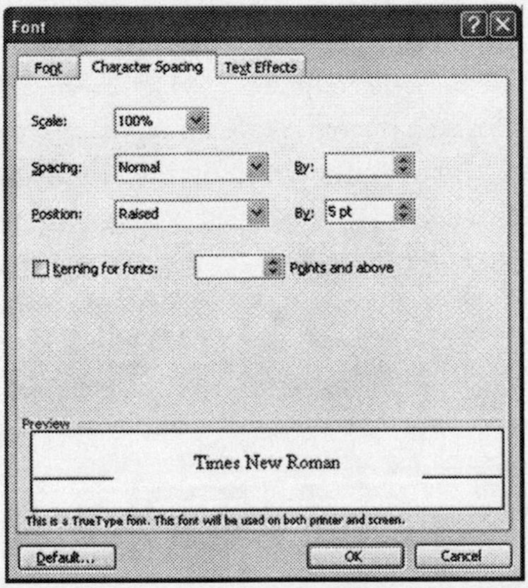

Figure 1-32

1.5.5   *Endnotes*

Endnotes appear at the end of chapters or end of the entire dissertation. Like footnotes, they contain bibliographic information or narrative text. Some dissertations use both endnotes and footnotes, although most use one or the other or neither.

Word 2003 comes with a built-in style for endnotes, which you can modify to suit the requirements of your dissertation format rules. Click on **Format** and then on **Styles and Formatting.** In the **Styles and Formatting** pane, be sure that the **Show** drop-down menu is set to **All Styles.** Under **Pick formatting to apply**, look for an entry for **Endnote Text.** (If there is no listing for **Endnote Text,** set **Show** to **Custom...** to open the **Format Settings** dialog box. Under **Styles to be visible,** click in the box in front of **Endnote Text** so that a check mark appears in the box. Set the **Category** drop-down menu to **All styles** and click on **OK** to close the **Format Settings** dialog box.)

Then right-click on the **Endnote Text** style and select **Modify.**

First, set the typeface characteristics for your endnotes. On the **Modify Style** page, click on the **Format** button and then on **Font.** On the **Font** page, set the font characteristics for your endnotes. Many universities require endnotes to be the same font and point size as body text, so these are usually safe choices. Some universities do permit endnotes to be in a smaller point size than the body text. As always, check your style manual to be sure. Click **OK** when you're done with the font characteristics, which returns you to the **Modify Style** dialog box. Do not click **OK** yet in the **Modify Style** dialog box.

Example: Your university requires that endnotes be of the same font and point size as body text. Suppose your body text uses 12-point Times New Roman. Figure 1-33 shows how to configure the endnote font.

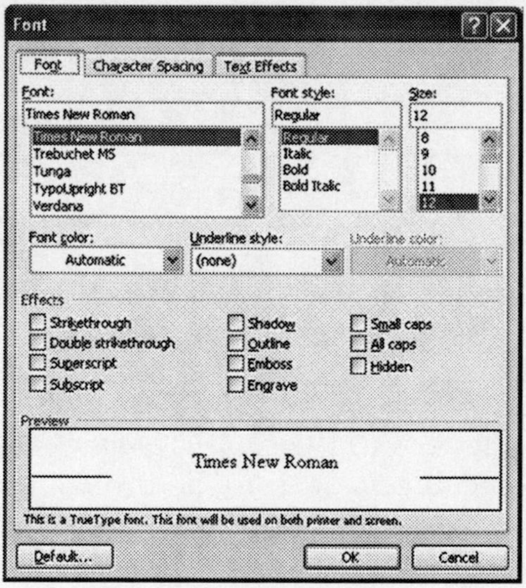

Figure 1-33

Next, set the line spacing for your endnotes. Some universities demand that endnotes be double-spaced; others permit single spacing. Click **Format** and then click on **Paragraph**. In the **Paragraph** dialog box, click on the **Indents and Spacing** tab.

In the **General** section under **Alignment,** pick **Left** from the drop-down menu, unless your dissertation uses fully justified text (section 1.3.1.3), in which case you should select **Justified**.

In the **Indentation** section, set **Left** and **Right** to **0 pt**. Under **Special**, pick **(none)** from the drop-down menu if you do not want the first line of the endnote text indented. If you do want the first line indented, pick **First line** and set **By** to the amount of indentation you want (generally, 0.5" works well). If you want the second and subsequent lines of every endnote item to be indented, select **Hanging** and set **By** to the desired amount of indentation (again, 0.5" works well).

In the **Spacing** section of the dialog box, set **Before** to **0 pt**. Set **After** to **0 pt** if you do not want any blank space between endnotes. If you want a single line of space between each endnote, enter the point size of your body font, that is, **10 pt** if you're using a 10-point font and **12 pt** if you're using a 12-point font. If you want 1.5 lines of space between footnotes, use **15 pt** for 10-point type and **18 pt** for 12-point type.

From the **Line spacing** drop-down menu, select the required line spacing for endnotes (usually either **Single** or **Double**). Leave **At** blank. (But if you're using Word's **Exactly** setting, select **Exactly** from the drop-down menu and set **At** to **10 pt** for single-spaced 10-point type, **15 pt** for 10-point type with 1.5-line spacing, **20 pt** for double-spaced 10-point type, **12 pt** for single-spaced 12-point type, **18 pt** for 12-point type with 1.5-line spacing, and **24 pt** for double-spaced 12-point type.) Click **OK**.

Example: At the University of Wisconsin at Madison, endnotes may be single spaced with an extra line of space between notes. Figure 1-34 shows how to configure this if you are using 12-point type.

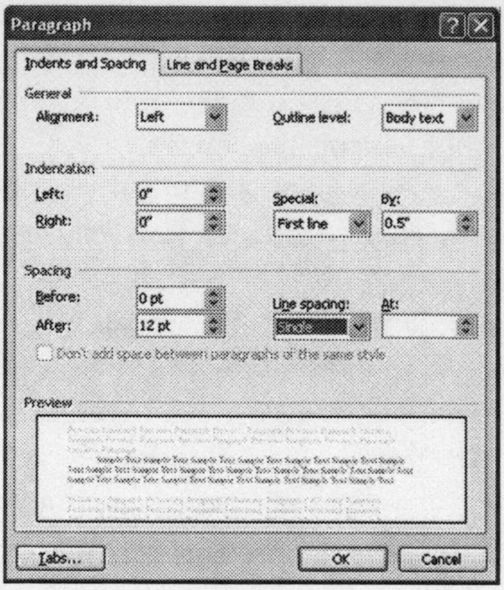

Figure 1-34

After you click **OK** on the **Paragraph** dialog box, you return to the **Modify Style** dialog box. You may wish to create a keyboard shortcut for this style (see section 1.4.1.4). When you're done, click **OK** in the **Modify Style** dialog box, and your endnote style is ready for you to use.

1.5.6   Endnote separators

As it does for footnotes, Word 2003 provides three elements for separating endnotes from regular text:

1.   The *endnote separator,* which Word inserts between the end of the body text and the first line of endnotes. The default value is a 2-inch unindented line.

2.   The *endnote continuation separator,* which is used at the top of the second and subsequent pages of endnotes. The default value is a line from the left margin to the right margin.

3.   The *endnote continuation notice,* which is also used when an endnote continues from one page to another. The notice is placed after the last line of the part of the endnote that fits on the first page. The default value is to have no continuation notice.

Unlike the case of footnotes, you may well want to change (or eliminate) these endnote separators. To do so, however, you must have inserted at least one endnote into your document. To insert the endnote, put your cursor anywhere in the body of your template document. Click on **Insert**, then **Reference**, then **Footnote**. The **Footnote and Endnote** dialog box will come up. Under **Location**, click **Endnotes** (Figure 1-35) and then click **Insert**. If you have the template open in the **Normal** view, the **Endnotes** pane opens at the bottom of the page (Figure 1-36). From the **Endnotes** drop-down menu, select **Endnote Separator** or **Endnote Continuation Separator** or **Endnote Continuation Notice**, depending on which you want to modify. The desired separator appears in the **Endnotes** pane (Figure 1-37 depicts the endnote continuation separator). Modify it or delete it, as you wish. Click on another separator if you wish to do more modifications, or click **Close** when you're done. Finally, be sure to delete the endnote number from your text at this stage; the endnote will be deleted, but the changes to the separators or continuation notice will be retained.

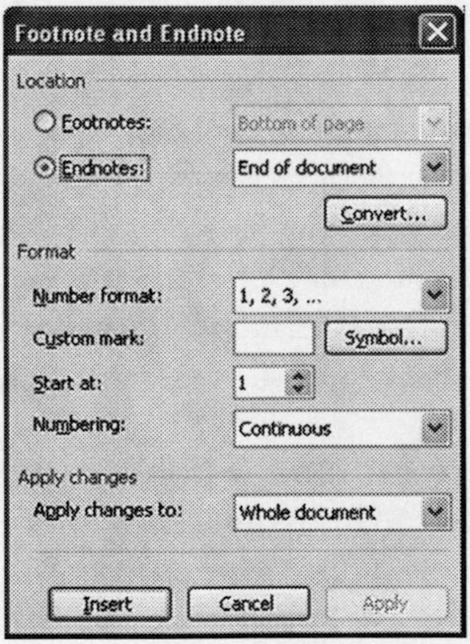

Figure 1-35

Figure 1-36

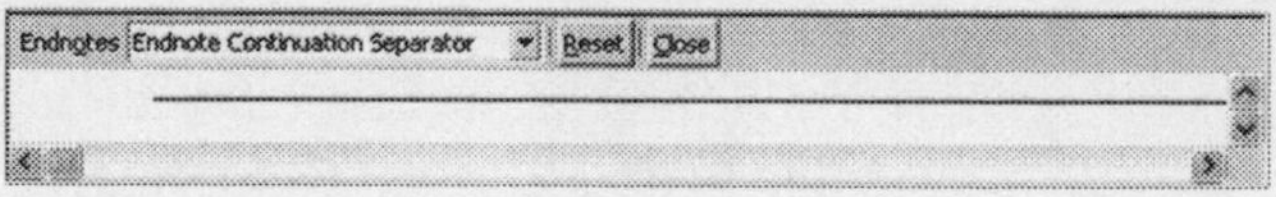

Figure 1-37

1.5.7   Endnote numbers

As was the case with footnote numbers (see section 1.5.4), Word 2003 may generate endnote numbers that are too small for your institution. To create endnote numbers in a larger point size, follow the procedure described in section 1.5.4—but make the change this time to the **Endnote Reference** style, not the **Footnote Reference** style. You must also adjust line spacing to **Exactly** in order to prevent Word 2003 from adding extra space before a line that includes an endnote number. See section 1.3.1.1.

1.5.8   Bibliography

A bibliography lists sources that are cited by a dissertation. Most dissertations have a bibliography. However, there are third-party programs that can make the compilation and formatting of a bibliography much easier than doing it by hand. If you are using such a program, you can skip this section, because your third-party program can handle formatting for you.

Word 2003 does not come with a built-in style for bibliographies, so we must create one. Click on **Format** and then **Styles and Formatting** to bring up the **Styles and Formatting** task pane. Click on the **New Style** button.

In the **New Style** dialog box, enter the name **Bibliography** in the **Name** field (Figure 1-38). For **Style type**, pick **Paragraph** from the pull-down menu. For **Style based on**, pick **Normal** from the pull-down menu, and for **Style for following paragraph**, pick **Normal** from the pull-down menu. Be sure the **Automatically update** box is *not* checked.

To set the margins and line spacing for your bibliography, click **Format** and click on **Paragraph**. In the **Paragraph** dialog box, click on the **Indents and Spacing** tab.

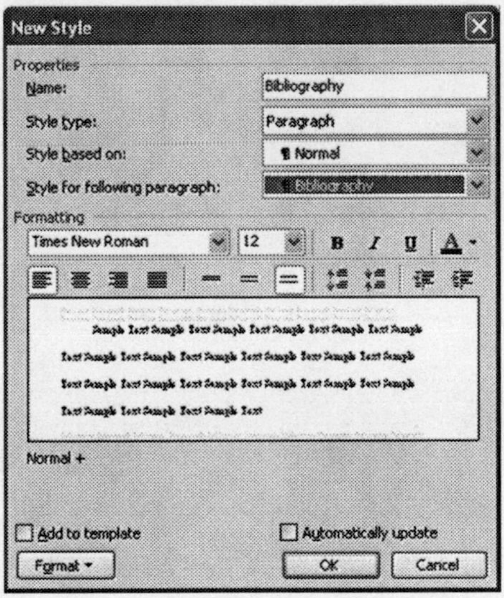

Figure 1-38

In the **General** section under **Alignment**, pick **Left** from the drop-down menu, unless your dissertation uses fully justified text (section 1.3.1.3), in which case you should select **Justified**. In the **Indentation** section, set **Left** and **Right** to **0"** (most universities do not require that bibliography entries have inset margins). If your style requires that the first line of a bibliography entry be indented, pick **First line** from the **Special** drop-down menu, and then set **By** to the required indentation (usually, **0.5"** is acceptable). If your style requires a hanging indent—that is, the first line of each bibliography entry is flush left and the rest of the lines of the entry are indented by a specified amount—pick **Hanging** from the **Special** drop-down menu and set **By** to the desired indentation (usually **0.5"**). If your style does not require a paragraph indentation at the start of every bibliography entry, pick **(none)** from the **Special** drop-down menu.

Example: Turabian's *A Manual for Writers of Term Papers, Theses, and Dissertations* calls for each bibliography entry to be flush left, with additional lines indented five spaces. A 0.5" hanging indent is a reasonable approximation of the five-space requirement. Figure 1-39 shows how to configure this line spacing.

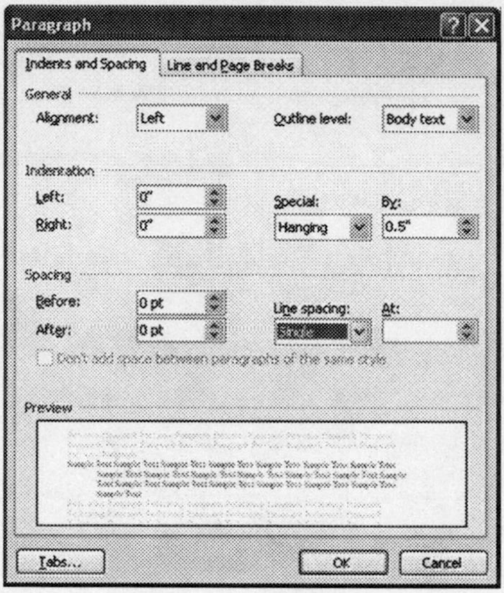

Figure 1-39

In the **Spacing** section of the dialog box, select the desired line spacing for the inside of each bibliography entry from the **Line spacing** drop-down menu and leave **At** blank. (But if you're using Word's **Exactly** setting, select **Exactly** from the drop-down menu and set **At** to **10 pt** for single-spaced 10-point type, **15 pt** for 10-point type with 1.5-line spacing, **20 pt** for double-spaced 10-point type, **12 pt** for single-spaced 12-point type, **18 pt** for 12-point type with 1.5-line spacing, and **24 pt** for double-spaced 12-point type.)

Set Before to **0 pt** and set **After** to **0 pt** unless your university requires an extra line of space between each bibliography entry; if this is the case, enter **10** for 10-point type and **12** for 12-point type. Click **OK**.

Example: George Mason University requires that entries in a bibliography be single spaced, with double spaces between each entry. If you are using a 12-point font, Figure 1-40 shows how to set that up.

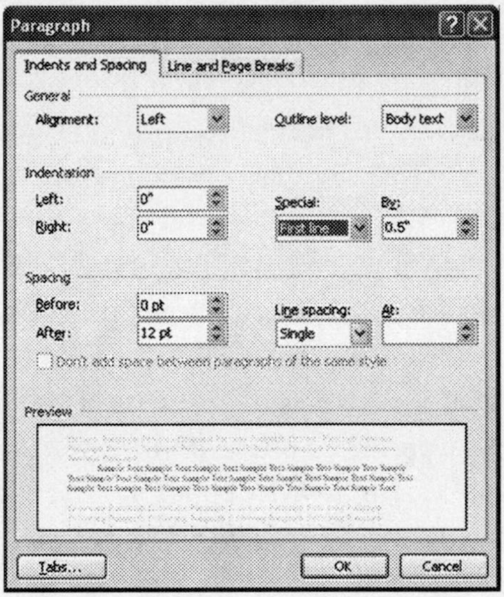

Figure 1-40

After you click **OK** on the **Paragraph** dialog box, you return to the **New Style** dialog box. You may wish to create a keyboard shortcut for this style (see section 1.4.1.4). When you're done, click **OK** in the **New Style** dialog box, and your bibliography style is ready for you to use.

1.5.9   Captions

If you plan to use figures or tables in your dissertation, you also need captions—Word's term for the title that accompanies a figure or table. With the captions style, you can set the font, font size, line spacing, and other characteristics of your captions.

To modify the captions style, click on **Format** and then on **Styles and Formatting** to bring up the **Styles and Formatting** task pane. In the **Styles and Formatting** pane, be sure that the **Show** drop-down menu is set to **All Styles**. Under **Pick formatting to apply,** look for an entry for **Caption.** (If there is no listing for **Caption,** set **Show** to **Custom...** to open the **Format Settings** dialog box. Under **Styles to be visible**, click in the box in front of **Caption** so that a check mark appears in the box. Set the **Category** drop-down menu to **All styles** and click on **OK** to close the **Format Settings** dialog box.)

Right-click on the **Caption** entry and then select **Modify** to bring up the **Modify Style** dialog box.

On the **Modify Style** page, click on the **Format** button and then on **Font**. On this page, set the font characteristics for your captions. Many universities require captions to be in the same font and point size as body text, so these are usually safe choices. Some universities do permit captions to be in a smaller point size than the body text. As always, check your style manual to be sure. Click the single-line icon from the **Underline style** drop-down menu if you want your caption to be underlined; select **Bold** or **Italic** for **Font style** if you want your captions to be in bold face or italic. Click **OK** when you're done with the font characteristics, which will return you to the **Modify Style** dialog box.

Then set the line spacing for your captions. Click the **Format** button in the lower left hand of the **Modify Style** dialog box and click on **Paragraph**. In the **Paragraph** dialog box, click on the **Indents and Spacing** tab.

In the **General** section, under **Alignment**, pick **Left** from the drop-down menu, unless your dissertation uses fully justified text (section 1.3.1.3), in which case you should select **Justified**. In the **Indentation** section, set **Left** and **Right** to **0"**. Under **Special**, pick **(none)** from the drop-down menu, unless you want the first line of each caption to be indented, in which case set **Special** to **First line** and **By** to the amount of the indentation.

In the **Spacing** section of the dialog box, set **Before** to **0 pt**. For **After**, if you want a single blank line between your major heading and the text that follows, enter the point size of your body font, that is, **10 pt** for 10-point font and **12 pt** for 12-point font. If you want 1.5 lines of space after the heading, set **After** to **15 pt** for 10-point type and **18 pt** for 12-point type.

From the **Line spacing** drop-down menu, select the required line spacing for captions; some universities demand that captions be single-spaced while others want them to have the same line spacing as your body text. Leave **At** blank. (But if you're using Word's **Exactly** setting, select **Exactly** from the drop-down menu and set **At** to **10 pt** for single-spaced 10-point type, **15 pt** for 10-point type with 1.5-line spacing, **20 pt** for double-spaced 10-point type, **12 pt** for single-spaced 12-point type, **18 pt** for 12-point type with 1.5-line spacing, and **24 pt** for double-spaced 12-point type.) Click **OK**.

Example: The University of Mississippi requires that table titles, figure titles, and captions be single-spaced. You also decide to add a single blank line between captions and subsequent text. Figure 1-41 depicts how to set that configuration for 12-point type.

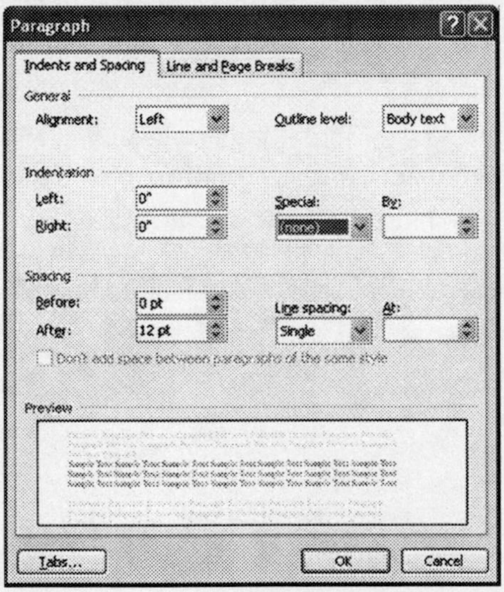

Figure 1-41

1.5.9.1 Chapter numbers in figure captions

By default, Word 2003 numbers figures sequentially, from 1 to the end of the dissertation. However, you may want each chapter's figures to be numbered separately, with Chapter 2's figures being Figure 2-1, Figure 2-2, and so forth.

To configure Word 2003 to number captions in this fashion, click on **Insert** and **Reference** and **Caption** to bring up the **Caption** dialog box (Figure 1-42). Select Figure from the **Options Label** drop-down menu. Then click on the **Numbering** button to bring up the **Caption Numbering** dialog box (Figure 1-43). Be sure the **Format** drop-down menu is set to **1, 2, 3, ...** and check the **Include chapter number** box. If you're following the style directions in this book, **Chapter starts with style** should be set to **Heading 1**, and **Use separator** should be set to the marker that you want between the chapter number and the figure number; options are **hyphen, period, colon, em-dash**, and **en-dash**. Click **OK** to close the **Caption Numbering** box and **Close** (not **OK**) to close the **Caption** box.

Note: Some universities require that if chapter-based numbering is used for figures, then the same approach must be used for tables, figures, maps, or any other numbered items in the dissertation. If so, you must repeat the process described in the previous paragraph for each other type of numbered item in your dissertation, selecting the type of numbered item (table, equation, etc.) from the **Options Label** drop-down menu in the **Caption** dialog box.

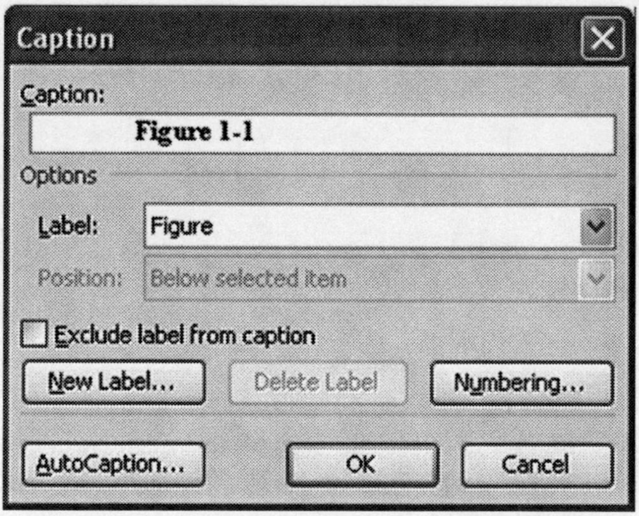

Figure 1-42

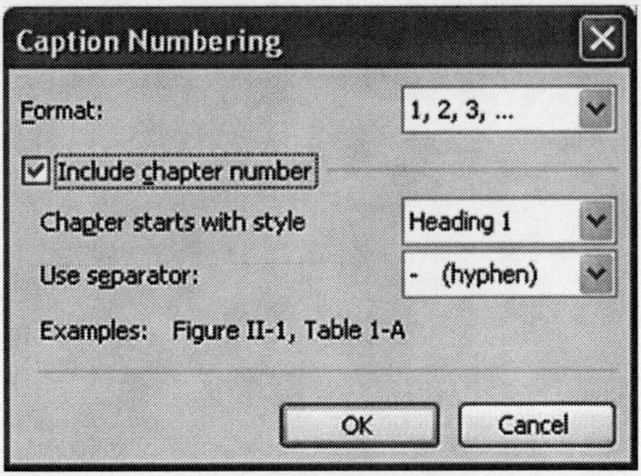

Figure 1-43

1.5.10 List styles

Sometimes you may want to include a numbered list in your dissertation. Short lists can usually be incorporated into the body text with no
special formatting required in Word 2003: "The directions were (1)
north, (2) south, (3) east, and (4) west." But lists with longer entries are
often rendered with each item as a separate paragraph, starting with a
number. Word 2003 can help in formatting these, but only if you configure it to format the lists according to the dictates of your style manual.
The *Publication Manual of the American Psychological Association,* for
example, requires that each item in a list start with a paragraph indent,
with the following lines flush left. Turabian's *A Manual for Writers of
Term Papers, Theses, and Dissertations* allows that format, but also
allows numbers to be flush left, with a hanging indent for the second
and subsequent lines.

To configure the default style that Word 2003 uses for numbered
lists, click on **Format,** then **Bullets and Numbering**, and then click on
the **Numbered** tab (Figure 1-44). Click on the numbering style that
suits you (and note that the styles can use letters as well as numbers,
so "Numbered" is really a bit of a misnomer).

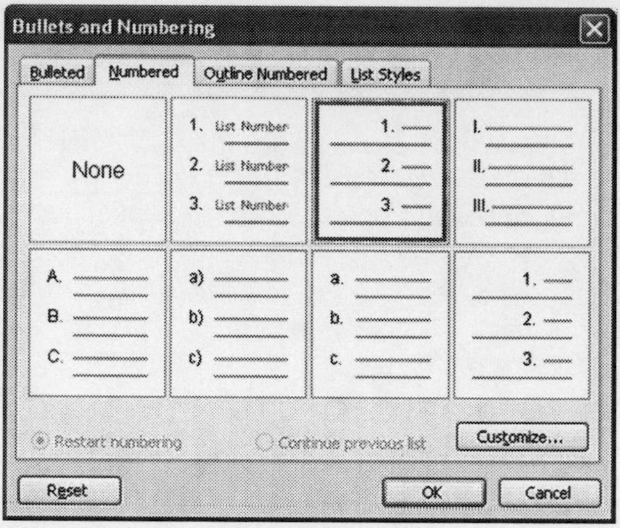

Figure 1-44

If you wish, you can modify any of the styles by clicking the **Customize** button. (**Customize** will be grayed out unless one of the numbering styles is selected.) This brings up the **Customize Numbered List** dialog box. Here you can change the number format (by typing text before the number or punctuation or other text after the number). Under **Number position**, select **Left** or **Centered** or **Right**. In the **Aligned at** box, enter the amount, in inches, that you want the number indented (or **0"** if you want no indent). In **Tab space after**, indicate the distance, in inches, that you want between the number and the start of the text. In **Indent at**, indicate the amount of indentation you want for the second and subsequent lines of an individual list entry. Click **OK** when you're done customizing the style. You will see a 1 (or an A, or I, or other symbol, depending on the numbering style that you selected). Delete the number or letter from the file that Word has open on your screen.

Example: The American Psychological Association calls for lists to have an indented number, with the second and following lines of each list entry flush left. Figure 1-45 shows how to revise the numbered-list style to conform to the psychological association's requirements.

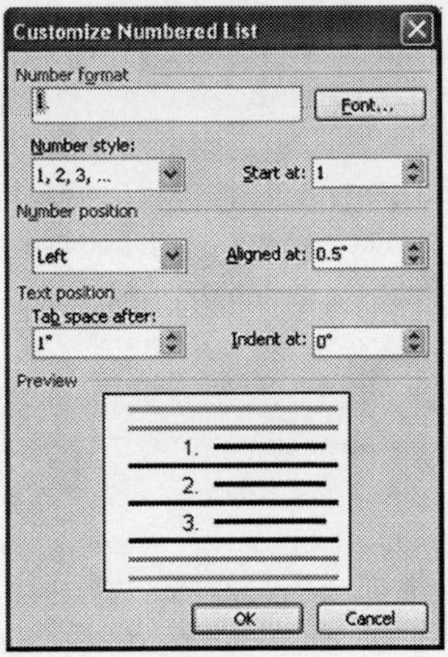

Figure 1-45

1.5.11 Page numbers

Although you've determined the location of page numbers on the pages of your dissertation, you haven't yet configured the font and font size of the page numbers. Word 2003 has a default setting for page numbers that is probably suitable for your use—but you should double-check to be sure.

Click on **Format** and then on **Styles and Formatting** to open the **Styles and Formatting** task pane. In the **Styles and Formatting** pane, be sure that the **Show** drop-down menu is set to **All Styles**. Scroll

through the **Pick formatting to apply** list until you find the entry
named **Page Number**. (If there is no listing for **Page Number,** set **Show**
to **Custom...** to open the **Format Settings** dialog box. Under **Styles to
be visible,** click in the box in front of **Page Number**, so that a check
mark appears in the box. Set the **Category** drop-down menu to **All
styles,** and click on **OK** to close the **Format Settings** dialog box.)

Right-click on the **Page Number** entry and select **Modify** from the
shortcut menu that appears. The **Modify Style** dialog box appears,
listing **Page Number** as the style's name. Be sure the **Automatically
update** box is *not* checked. Figure 1-46 shows the dialog box.

To set the typeface characteristics for your page numbers, on the
Modify Style page, click the **Format** button and then click **Font**. On
this page, select the font characteristics of your page number. It is
usually acceptable for the page number to be of the same font and
size as your body text. Some universities may permit the page number to be smaller than the body text. (Figure 1-47 shows how to configure the page number font as 12-point Times New Roman.) Click **OK**
when you're done setting your font requirements, to return to the
Modify Style page. Then click **OK** on the **Modify Style** page to save
your settings.

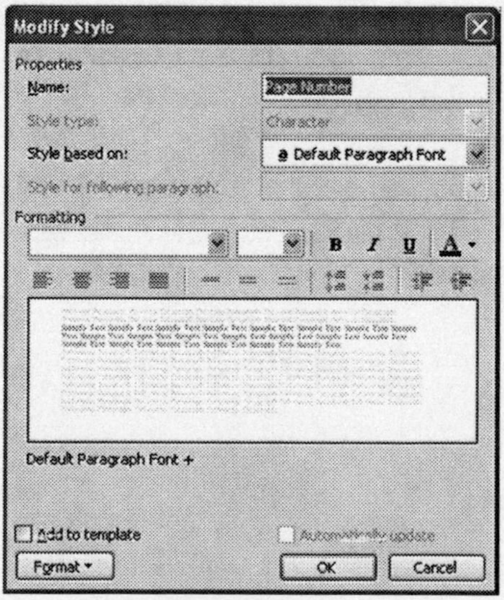

Figure 1-46

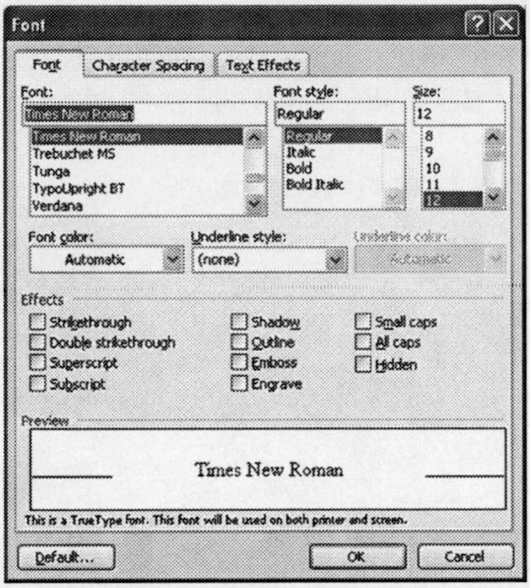

Figure 1-47

1.6   Double-checking your styles

At this point, the styles for your dissertation should be configured properly. But it never hurts to double-check. You can print out a list of all styles in your template by following these steps: From the **File** menu, click on **Print**. The **Print** dialog box comes up. From the **Print what** drop-down menu, select **Styles** and then click **OK** (Figure 1-48). You'll get a printout of all the styles in the template, so you can double-check them against your style manual.

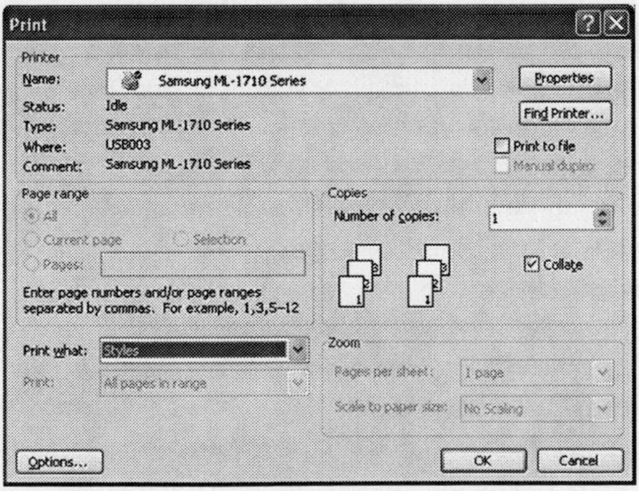

Figure 1-48

You can also print out a list of the keyboard shortcuts for formatting styles. From the **File** menu, click on **Print**. From the **Print what** drop-down menu, select **Key assignments** and click **OK** (Figure 1-49).

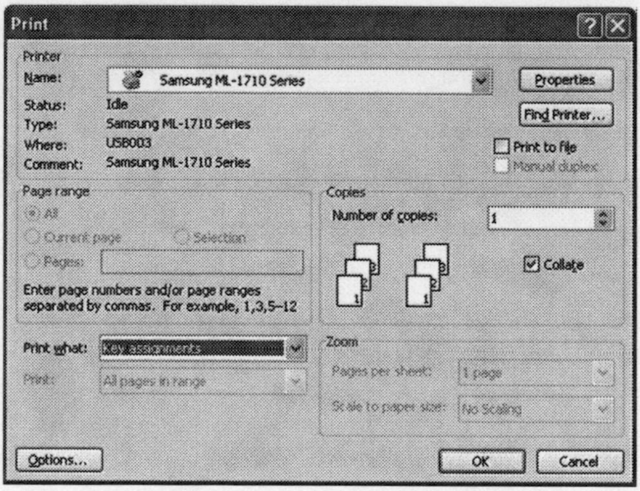

Figure 1-49

Keep these two lists handy as you prepare to write the body of your dissertation. They help you save time and stress.

1.7   Configuring AutoFormat

Word 2003 offers an automatic formatting option, called **AutoFormat**, that can automatically reformat text according to a variety of specifications, even as you are typing. Although this may sound innocuous, your institution's style rules may require you to turn off some of these options.

To configure **AutoFormat**, click on **Tools** and then **AutoCorrect Options** and finally the **AutoFormat** tab (Figure 1-50). Uncheck the boxes for any options that you wish to deactivate. Then click on the **AutoFormat as You Type** tab (Figure 1-51) and uncheck the same options here. Click **OK**.

Here are the options that AutoFormat offers:

"Straight quotes" with "smart quotes": Smart, or curly, quotes curve in the correct direction at the start and end of a quotation, but straight quotes are vertical. If this box is checked, Word 2003 uses a smart quote mark whenever you hit the single or double quotation mark key.

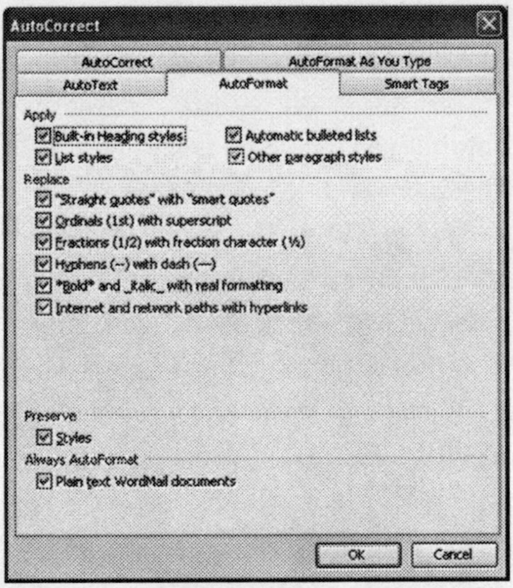

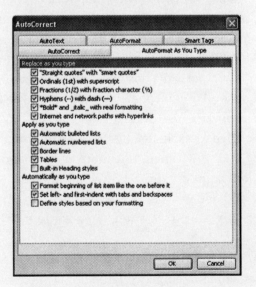

Figure 1-50

Figure 1-51

Ordinals (1st) with superscript: If this option is checked, AutoFormat converts ordinal numbers (1st, 2nd, 3rd) to superscripted versions (1st, 2nd, 3rd). However, some style manuals, like the *Publication Manual of the American Psychological Association,* do not call for superscripts with ordinals. If you're following such a style manual, make sure that this box is unchecked.

Fractions (1/2) with fraction character (½): If this option is checked, AutoFormat converts the characters 1/4, 1/2, and 3/4 to ¼, ½, and ¾ respectively. This does not work with other fractions, even if they're available in the font that you're using.

Hyphens (-) with dash (—): Em dashes are the long dashes that are used to set off a phrase from the main clause of a sentence. If you check this box, AutoFormat watches for whenever you hit the hyphen key twice in a row and replaces the hyphens with a single, long dash, called an "en dash." Similarly, it replaces three hyphens in a row with an even longer dash, called an "em dash." But some style manuals, like the *Publication Manual of the American Psychological Association,* mandate that em dashes should be represented in the text as two hyphens. If you're following such a style manual, make sure that this box is unchecked.

Bold and _italic_ with real formatting: If this box is checked, whenever you type an asterisk followed by a word or phrase and then followed by another asterisk, Word 2003 converts that word or phrase to bold (and eliminates the asterisks). Using the underscore character (_) underlines the text. This is a convenient way to format text.

Hyperlinks: If you check the box next to **Internet and network paths with hyperlinks,** AutoFormat spots whenever you type a URL (such as *http://chronicle.com*) or a network path (such as C:\Program Files) and converts that to a hyperlink. In default Word 2003 formatting, hyperlinks are in blue text and underlined, but many style manuals expect that URLs and network paths are treated the same way as regular text—that is, in black type and not underlined. If you wish to avoid this type of special formatting in your dissertation, be sure that this box remains unchecked.

(**Caveat:** Options for **AutoFormat** and **AutoFormat as You Type** are not stored in a document template. Rather, they are stored in your computer's registry. So if you move your dissertation template to a new computer and open it there, you have to reconfigure AutoFormat.)

1.8 Saving your template

When you've completed configuring your template, you must save it. Click on **File** and **Save As**. In the dialog box, type a name for the template (here, and throughout the book, we call it **My Dissertation**), and from the

Save as type pull-down menu, select **Document Template** (Figure 1-52). Click on **OK**.

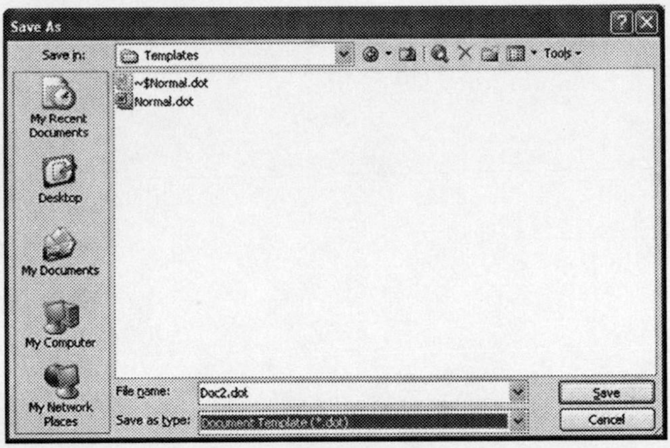

Figure 1-52

1.9   Revising your template

You can change your template at any time. First, you must know the template's location. Click on **Tools** and then **Options** and then on the **File Locations** tab. **User templates** lists the directory in which templates are stored by default. (If the pathname won't fit in the allotted space, it will be truncated by an ellipsis. You can double-click on the **User templates** line to get into the actual directory. By navigating upward through the file system, you can determine the full path. Click **Cancel** when you've deduced the full path.)

Click OK to exit the **Options** dialog box. Then, from the **File** menu, click on **Open**. From the **Files of type** pull-down menu, pick **Document Templates**. Use the **Look in** box and navigate to the location of your Word 2003 templates folder. Click on the desired template file. After making any revisions, be sure to save the revised template, following the instructions in section 1.8. Also, be sure to change **Files of type** back to **All Files**.

1.10 Congratulations!

You've finished configuring your template, and you've stored it in the proper location so that you can use it as the starting point for your chapters and other major sections of your dissertation.

Chapter 2

Formatting chapters

Each chapter of your dissertation should be in a separate Word file, at least until you are ready to merge the various parts together into a final document. This approach allows you to easily share individual chapters with committee members and fellow graduate students. It also minimizes the risk of losing your entire dissertation if a file is corrupted.

2.1 Creating from scratch

In many respects, the best way to create a new chapter is from scratch in a new Word file, using the dissertation template that you crafted in Chapter 1. This approach ensures that your chapter will be correctly formatted in all respects from the very start, saving you potential headaches in reformatting.

To create a new dissertation chapter, click on **File** and then **New** to get the **New Document** pane. In the **Templates** section, click once on **On my computer** to get the **Templates** dialog box. If you followed the instructions on saving your template in section 1.8, the **General** tab should include an icon labeled **My Dissertation** (see Figure 2-1). Double-click on this icon, and Word 2003 will create a new document based on the template named **My Dissertation**.

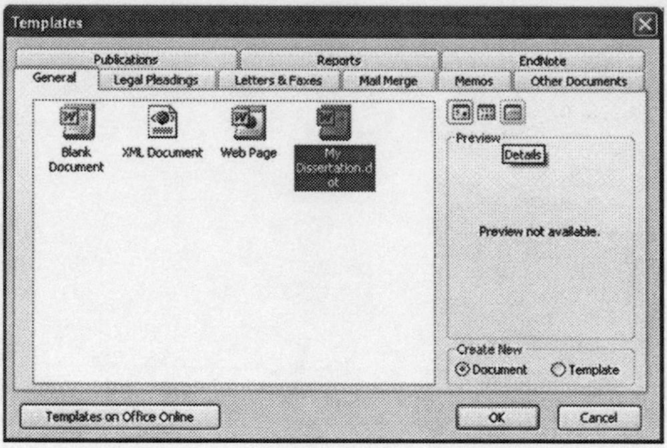

Figure 2-1

2.1.1   Chapter title

Start by adding your chapter title. Type it as the first line of the file. Then, before hitting **Enter**, either type the shortcut key for the Heading 1 style (see section 1.4.1.4) or select **Heading 1** from the style drop-down menu in the **Formatting** toolbar (Figure 2-2). The text will be reformatted according to your dictates for the selected style. Now hit **Enter**.

Figure 2-2

You may want your chapter title to occupy two lines. For example, you may want the first line to be "Chapter 1" and the second line to be "Literature Review." To accomplish this, type the first line but do not press **Enter**. Instead, press **Shift** and **Enter** simultaneously at the end of the first line. Then type the second line. At the end of the second line, either type the shortcut key for the **Heading 1** style or select **Heading 1** from the style drop-down menu in the **Formatting** toolbar. Then hit **Enter** at the end of the second line. This will ensure that the entire chapter title is formatted correctly and that it appears in full in the table of contents (section 7.3).

2.1.2   Chapter body

Now you can add the body of your chapter. As you type, you can add major headings and minor headings (see sections 1.4.2 and 1.4.3) by typing each on its own line. Before you hit **Enter**, either type the shortcut key for the heading style that you want to use or select the style name from the style drop-down menu in the **Formatting** toolbar. The text will be reformatted immediately. Touch **Enter**.

For adding tables to your text, see Chapter 3; for adding figures, see Chapter 4; and for adding equations, see Chapter 5.

2.1.3   Adding existing text

You can import text from another document, such as your dissertation proposal. One option is to insert an entire document into your chapter—if the document is a Word document, is a plain text file, or is in rich text format. To do this, place your cursor at the point in your chapter where you want the material to be inserted. Then click on **Insert** and **File**. Use the **Insert File** dialog box to navigate to the location of the file that you want to add to the chapter (Figure 2-3). You may need to adjust the selection from the **Files of type** drop-down menu to the type of file that you are seeking. Click **Insert**, and the contents of the file will be added to the chapter, with the original version of the file left unchanged.

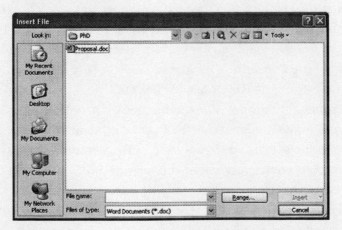

Figure 2-3

If your material is in a file of a different type (such as a WordPerfect file), you can open the file with the program that created it and copy the desired material to the Windows Clipboard (usually by selecting the material and then clicking **Edit** and **Copy**). Then open your dissertation chapter in Word 2003 and place your cursor where you want the material to go. Click on **Edit** and then **Paste**.

Unfortunately, when you add material in this manner, it is not always automatically reformatted to conform to your dissertation template. So you must examine the added material carefully. At any major or minor heading, position the cursor somewhere within the heading and format it: Either type the shortcut key for the heading style that you want to use or select the style name from the style drop-down menu in the **Formatting** toolbar.

Also, check that the page margins remain correct: Click on **File** and **Page Setup** and then on the **Margins** tab of the **Page Setup** dialog box. Check to be sure that the margins are the same as what you set in section 1.1.1. If they are incorrect, change them to the correct values. Click **OK** to exit.

Be sure, too, that your new material is of the same font type and size that you have chosen for the dissertation. You can determine what font is in use at any point in your document by looking at the **Formatting** toolbar (see Figure 2-2). It lists the font and font size in effect at the cursor. Scroll through your new material, checking to be sure that the font and font size are correct. To reformat text, highlight the text that you want to change and select the desired font and font size from the **Formatting** toolbar or click on **Format** and **Font,** make selections from the **Font** tab, and click **OK.**

If page numbers are in the wrong location, delete the page numbers and reinsert them correctly. To delete the incorrectly positioned page numbers, click on **View** and then **Header and Footer** to get the **Header and Footer** toolbar. At the top and bottom of the page, you will see a dashed area representing the header and footer for the page. Determine whether the header or footer box contains the incorrectly positioned page number: It will contain the page number on a gray background (see Figure 2-4). Highlight the page number and then press the **Delete** key to delete it; click **Close** on the **Header and Footer** toolbar. Now insert page numbers in the correct location, following the instructions in section 1.2.

Figure 2-4

If you suffer nagging problems that you have difficulty solving, another option is to intentionally lose all formatting in the material as you paste it into Word and then manually reformat it. To do this, when you paste a copied selection into Word, select **Paste Special** rather than **Paste** from the **Edit** menu. From the **Paste Special** dialog box (Figure 2-5), select **Unformatted Text** from the **As** menu and then click **OK**. The pasted material will lose all its original formatting, so you will have to manually reformat major and minor headings and block quotations. You may also have to reformat body text with the **Normal** format. However, the page margins and page numbering in your document should remain correct.

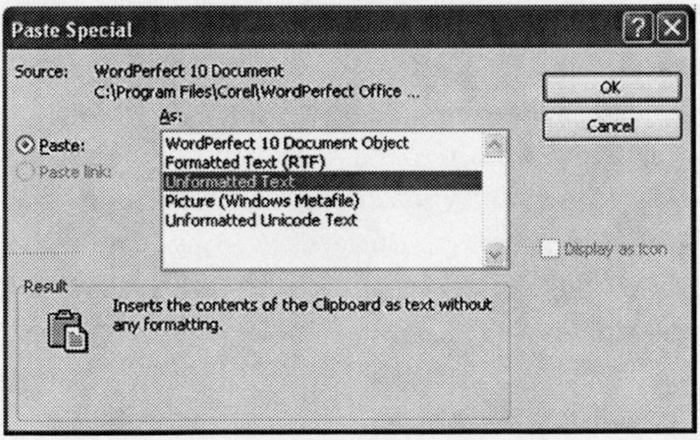

Figure 2-5

2.2   Reformatting an existing document

There's a second approach that you can take to preparing the Word files for your dissertation: You can reformat one or more existing Word files—your dissertation proposal, for example—into the proper format for a dissertation chapter. Here's how: Open the document. Click on

Tools and then **Templates and Add-Ins** (Figure 2-6). Click the **Attach** button, and in the **Attach Template** dialog box, navigate to the location of your **Dissertation** template (see section 1.8).

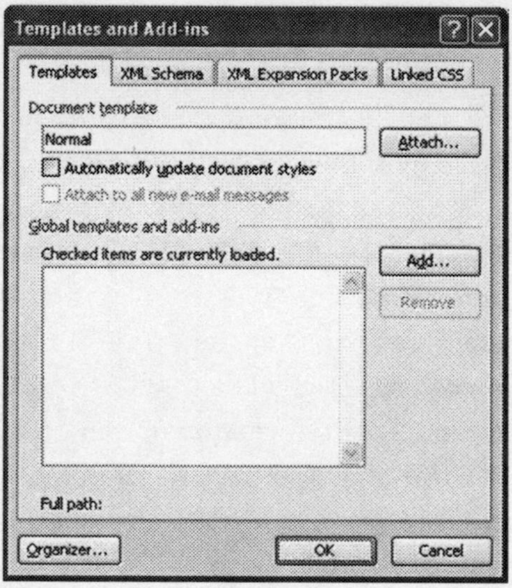

Figure 2-6

Click **Open** to return to the **Templates and Add-Ins** dialog box. Check the **Automatically update document styles** box. Click **OK**.

This will apply the styles in your dissertation template to the document that is open. But you should scroll through the document to double-check that the formatting is correct. However, this procedure will not revise margins or page numbering, so you should verify that they are correct and make changes as needed (see section 2.1.3).

2.3 Block quotations

To add a block quotation to your text, type the quotation as its own paragraph (most style manuals call for no quotation marks around a block quotation). Before you hit the Enter key, either type the shortcut key for the **Blockquote** style (see section 1.5.1) or select **Blockquote** from the style drop-down menu in the **Formatting** toolbar. The text will be reformatted as directed. Now you can hit **Enter** and continue with your typing.

2.4   Creating references in your text

Three major types of reference citations are used in dissertations:

1. In-text notes, such as those called for by the *Publication Manual of the American Psychological Association*, in which the author's last name and year of publication are printed in the text, corresponding to an entry in a reference list at the end of the dissertation.
2. Footnotes, which are signaled by a superscript number in the text, corresponding to a footnote printed at the bottom of the page.
3. Endnotes, which are signaled by a superscript number in the text, corresponding to an endnote printed at the end of the chapter or the dissertation.

Consider using third-party bibliographic software—such as EndNote, ProCite, or RefWorks—to help you manage your references. They will make sure that the references are formatted correctly and that your bibliography (if you have one) contains every reference that is cited in the text.

2.4.1   Creating in-text notes

Creating in-text notes is easy, because they usually are just ordinary text. Some use the author's name and publication year, while others use the author's name and page number.

You can type these directly into your file, but if you're using a bibliographic program, have it add the note instead: Position your cursor at the point in your chapter where you want the note to appear and instruct the bibliographic program to deposit the note into the text (instructions vary by program).

2.4.2   Creating a footnote

To insert a footnote, put your cursor in your chapter where you want the superscript number to appear. Click on **Insert**, then **Reference**, and then **Footnote**. The **Footnote and Endnote** dialog box will come up (Figure 2-7). Under **Location**, click the **Footnotes** radio button, and from the adjacent drop-down menu pick the location for the footnotes. **Bottom of page** places the footnotes between the bottom margin and the footer, which is a location that is forbidden by most universities. **Below Text** keeps the footnotes above the bottom margin, so this is probably the setting that you want.

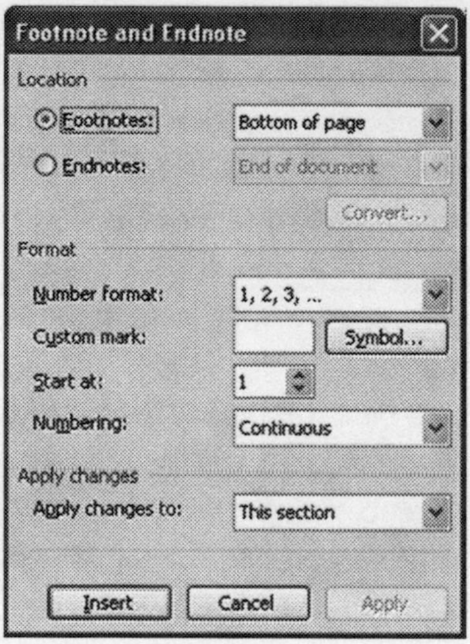

Figure 2-7

Be sure that **Number format** corresponds to your desired format (most likely, **1, 2, 3, ...**). Set the **Numbering** drop-down menu to **Continuous** if you want all footnotes in your document to be numbered from 1 to the end of the dissertation, **Restart Each Section** if you want each chapter's footnotes to be numbered separately, or **Restart Each Page** if you want each page's footnotes to be numbered separately starting at 1. Set **Apply Changes to Whole document.** Then click **Insert**. The footnote number (called the note reference mark) will be added to the text. If you have the file open in the **Print Layout** view (if necessary, to switch to **Print Layout** view, click on **View** and **Print Layout**), the **Footnotes** pane also will open at the bottom of the page, with the same superscript number as was just added to the text. Place your cursor next to this superscript number and either type in your footnote or direct your bibliographic program to insert the relevant note information (instructions vary by program). You can click **Close** to close the **Footnote** pane, but this is not required—you can move back to the body text by simply clicking your cursor in that part of the screen.

If you are using third-party bibliographic software, you should turn off any features through which the program automatically creates a bibliography as you write. Because you want the bibliography to appear at the end of the dissertation, not at the end of each chapter, using this feature will add an unwanted bibliography at the end of each chapter.

2.4.3   Creating an endnote

Creating an endnote is very similar to creating a footnote. First, put your cursor in your chapter where you want the superscript number to appear. Click on **Insert**, then **Reference**, and then **Footnote** (that's no typo—**Footnote** is correct). The **Footnote and Endnote** dialog box will come up (Figure 2-7).

Under **Location**, click the **Endnotes** radio button, and from the adjacent drop-down menu pick the location for the endnotes: **End of document,** if you want all endnotes from all chapters gathered together at the end of your dissertation, or **End of section,** if you want endnotes for a given chapter at the end of that chapter.

Note, however, that **End of section** will not work properly if your chapter includes landscape orientation pages or facing pages. In such arrangements, the landscape pages and facing pages are considered new sections, and so the endnotes for the part of the chapter that preceded the landscape page or facing page would be deposited just before the landscape page or facing page, not at the end of the chapter. Under such circumstances, you should collect your endnotes at the end of the dissertation or rotate your graphics so that they do not require a landscape page.

However, **End of document** suffers from its own problems, because many dissertations include information, such as appendices, that must follow the endnotes. To work around this problem, you can break your dissertation into two Word 2003 files: One would include all material from the start of the dissertation through the endnotes, and the second would include the material that is to appear after the endnotes. When printing this second section, be sure to set its starting page to the page number following the endnotes.

Be sure that **Number format** corresponds to your desired format (most likely, **1, 2, 3, ...**). Set the **Numbering** drop-down menu to **Continuous** if you want all endnotes in your document to be numbered from 1 to the end of the dissertation, or **Restart each section** if you want each chapter's endnotes to be numbered separately. Click **Insert**. The endnote number (called the note reference mark) will be added to the text; if you have the file open in the **Print Layout** view (if necessary, click on **View** and **Print Layout** to get into **Print Layout** view), the **Endnotes** pane also will open at the bottom of the page, with the same superscript number as was just added to the text. Place your cursor next to this superscript number and either type your endnote or direct your bibliographic program to insert the relevant note information (instructions vary by program). You can click **Close** to close the **Endnote** pane, but this is not required—you can move back to the body text by simply clicking your cursor in that part of the screen.

2.4.3.1   Endnotes page

If you selected **End of Section** above, Word 2003 will deposit the endnotes at the very end of the chapter. If you want a heading for the endnotes, such as "Notes," you should add it as the last words in the chapter file. (If you want it to appear in your table of contents, use the **Heading 2** format to create this heading.) Likewise, if you want the notes to start on their own new page, you should insert a manual page break before the heading. To insert a manual page break, position your cursor where you want the page break to appear. Then press **Ctrl** and **Enter** or click on **Insert** and **Break** and **Page break** and **OK**.

2.5   Lists

You can add lists in your dissertation using the list style that you configured for your template (section 1.5.10). Simply type each entry in the list as its own paragraph. Then highlight the entire text for the list and click the **Numbering** icon on the **Formatting** toolbar (Figure 2-8).

Figure 2-8

2.6   AutoText

AutoText is a feature of Word 2003 that tries to save you time by anticipating phrases and offering to complete the phrases for you. Its settings are stored in the document template.

To see how AutoText works, start typing the name of the current month. After you type several characters, a small box will appear with the full name of the month. If you hit **Enter**, AutoText will add the contents of that box to your file.

If you have words or phrases that you expect to use frequently in your dissertation, you can add them to your AutoText dictionary. One way is to click **Tools**, then **AutoCorrect Options**, and then the **AutoText** tab (Figure 2-9). Under **Enter AutoText entries here,** type the text that you want AutoText to recognize and then click **Add**. (If there is an entry that you wish to remove, highlight its entry in the listing by clicking on it and then click on **Delete**.) This procedure will not add any formatting (e.g., underlining, bold, or italics) or special characters to the words you add to AutoText.

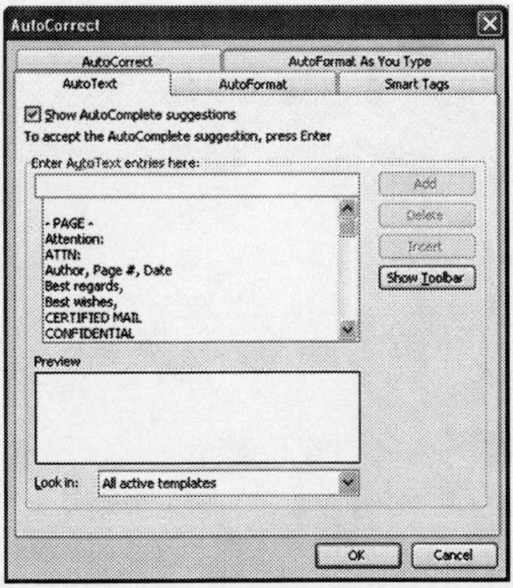

Figure 2-9

Or you can type the phrase in a Word file, highlight it, and then press the **Alt** and **F3** keys simultaneously. This will bring up a dialog box (Figure 2-10) asking you if you wish to add the phrase to **AutoText** (in this example, the highlighted word was "dissertation"). Click **OK**. (This approach allows you to add formatted text to the **AutoText** dictionary.)

Figure 2-10

To get a list of the AutoText entries for your current file, click on the **File** menu and then on **Print**. The **Print** dialog box will come up. From the **Print what** drop-down menu, select **AutoText entries** and then click **OK** (see Figure 2-11).

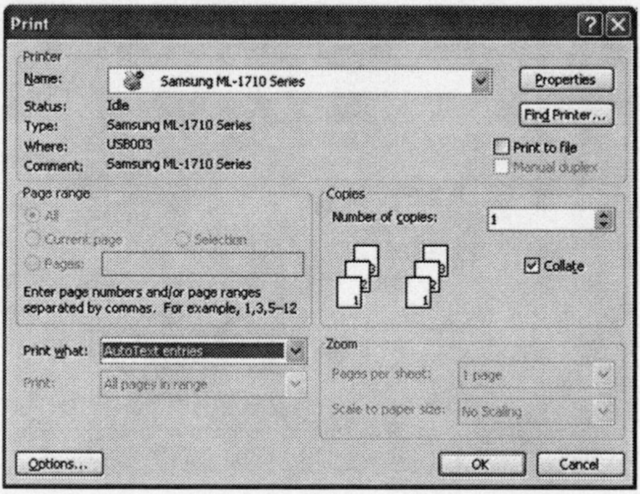

Figure 2-11

2.7   Symbols and special characters

You may need to use symbols or other characters that are not available on your computer keyboard. Windows and Word 2003 offer several ways to insert these into your document.

One way to add such a symbol is to click on the **Insert** menu and then on **Symbol**. You will get the **Symbol** dialog box (Figure 2-12). The **Symbols** tab of the dialog box shows all the symbols and special characters that you can add. Below the available symbols is a row containing all the symbols that you have recently used. (This listing is convenient for repeating a symbol you already have invoked.) To add a symbol, click twice on the symbol in the symbol table or in the list of recently used symbols. Or click once on the symbol and then click on the **Insert** button. Click **Close** or **Cancel** (your dialog box will show one or the other) when you are done.

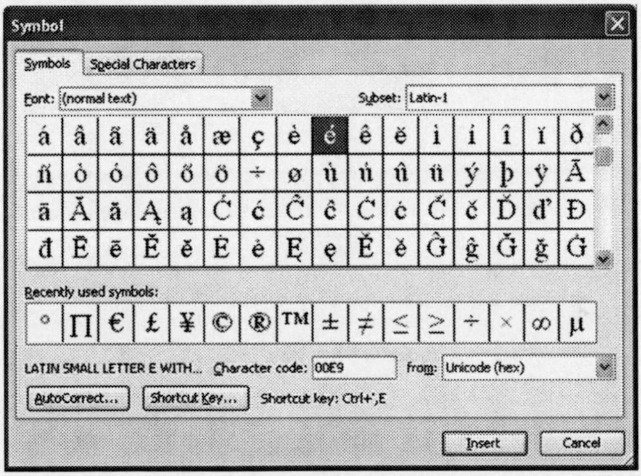

Figure 2-12

A second way to add special characters is through **AutoCorrect**, a Word 2003 facility that can be programmed to replace any string of characters with another string of characters (including special characters and symbols). For example, the default setting for **AutoCorrect** is to convert the three-character string (c) into the copyright symbol ©. First, be sure that **AutoCorrect** is active: Click **Tools** and then **AutoCorrect Options** and then the **AutoCorrect** tab, make sure that the box **Replace text as you type** is checked, and then click **OK.** Then, to enter the copyright symbol, all you need do is type **(c),** which will be rendered in your file as ©. You can see a list of your **AutoCorrect** abbreviations by clicking on **Tools** and then **AutoCorrect Options** and then the **AutoCorrect** tab (Figure 2-13).

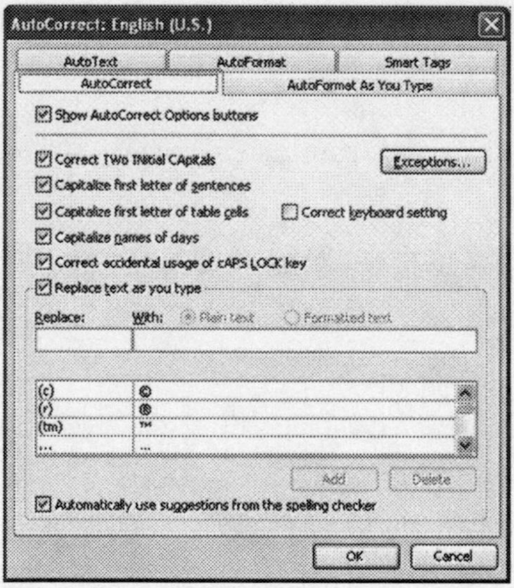

Figure 2-13

If you expect to use a particular symbol frequently, you may wish to add it to the **AutoCorrect** dictionary. In the **Replace** box, type the characters that you wish to replace in your text. In the **With** box, type the new characters that you wish to replace the old. Click the **Add** button and then **OK.** You can add text with special formatting as well: Type the text, with the special formatting, in a Word file, and highlight it. Then click on **Tools** and **AutoCorrect Options**. The highlighted text will appear in the **With** box; click the **Formatted text** radio button to instruct **AutoCorrect** that you want the replacement to include formatting. Type an entry in the **Replace** box; click **Add** and **OK.**

A third way to add a special character is by typing the symbol's key code—essentially, the symbol's numerical representation in Microsoft Windows—directly into Word 2003. (Because this is a feature of Windows, rather than solely of Word 2003, this approach can be used in many other programs that run in Windows.) A list of Windows keyboard codes can be found in the Appendix of this book. Be sure the cursor is at the location in your file where you want to insert the special character. Check that the **Num Lock** light on your keyboard is on, to activate the numeric keyboard on the right of your keyboard. Then, while holding down the **ALT** key, use the numeric keyboard (not the number keys at the top of your keyboard) to type **0** followed by the three-number code selected from the Appendix. For example, to enter the copyright symbol in this fashion, you would hold down the **ALT** key and type **0169** on the numeric keyboard.

2.8   Cross-references

At one point in your dissertation text, you may want to make reference to another portion of your text. For example, you may want to cite a specific table or perhaps another section of your dissertation. Although you can enter those cross-references manually, they could change if portions of your text get rearranged: For example, what had been Table 7 might become Table 8 if a new table is added. Word 2003 provides a way to add cross-references that it can revise as necessary.

To add a cross-reference, click **Insert** and then **Reference** and then **Cross-reference**. The **Cross-reference** dialog box will come up (Figure 2-14), providing a list of all elements for which you can create a cross-reference. From the **Reference type** drop-down menu, select a category, such as **Heading** or **Table**. The **For which heading** box will list elements that are available of that type; if the box is empty, you have not yet added any headings to the file. From the **Insert reference to** drop-down menu, you can select the specific type of reference that you want added: the table number or the table's caption (title), for example. Click **Insert** to add the cross-reference to your text. For example, if you wanted your text to say "as depicted in Table 2," you could type "as depicted in," followed by a space, and then insert a cross-reference to Table 2.

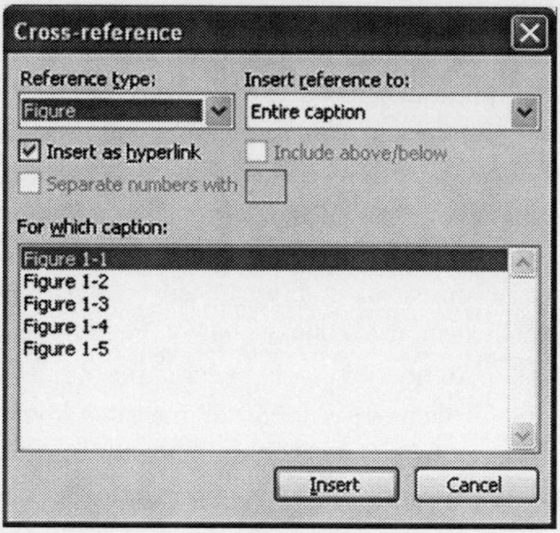

Figure 2-14

On your monitor, the cross-reference in the text will have a gray background, rather than the usual white background. This is Word's way of signaling that the cross-reference is not normal text but rather a "field," or a repository of information that can be updated as needed. (When printed, however, the field will appear without the gray background, like all other normal text in the document.)

Note: If you plan to make cross-references between different Word files—for example, between different dissertation chapters, each of which is a separate Word file—you must open the files simultaneously, either by merging the documents together (section 8.1) or though a master document (section 8.2), before adding the cross-references. In such a case, you may want to wait to insert the cross-references until you have finished the chapters and have merged them.

2.9   Facing pages

In most dissertations, the text appears only on right-hand pages of the bound volume, unlike a printed book, in which text appears on both the left- and right-hand pages. Occasionally, you may want to create a left-hand page with text on it as well as a right-hand page of text. This type of left-hand page is known as a "facing page." For example, you might want the facing page to contain the title of an illustration that occupies the entire right-hand page.

A challenge arises, however, because most graduate schools want the facing page in a dissertation to have the mirror-opposite layout of a standard page. For example, if standard pages have page numbers in the upper right hand corner, the facing page would have its page number in the upper left hand corner. Similarly, if standard pages have an extra-wide left margin, a facing page would have to have that extra-wide margin on its right side.

To create a facing page, place your cursor at the point in the document where the facing page is to start. From the **File** menu, click **Page Setup** and then the **Margins** tab. The values for the margins should be correct, as entered, for standard pages in your document. In the **Pages** section, select **Mirror margins** from the drop-down menu. From the **Apply to** drop-down menu, pick **This point forward.** Click **OK**. (Do not click **Default**.) Figure 2-15 shows the settings.

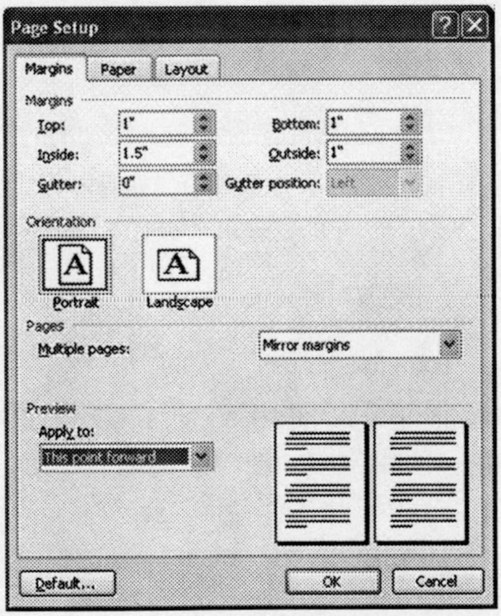

Figure 2-15

Now enter the text or other material for the facing page. When done, return the document to its previous page setting with normal margins: From the **File** menu, click **Page Setup** and then the **Margins** tab. The values for the margins should be correct, as entered, for standard pages in your document. In the **Pages** section, select **Normal** from the drop-down menu. From the **Apply to** drop-down menu, pick **This point forward.** Click **OK**. (Do not click **Default**.) Figure 2-16 depicts the dialog box.

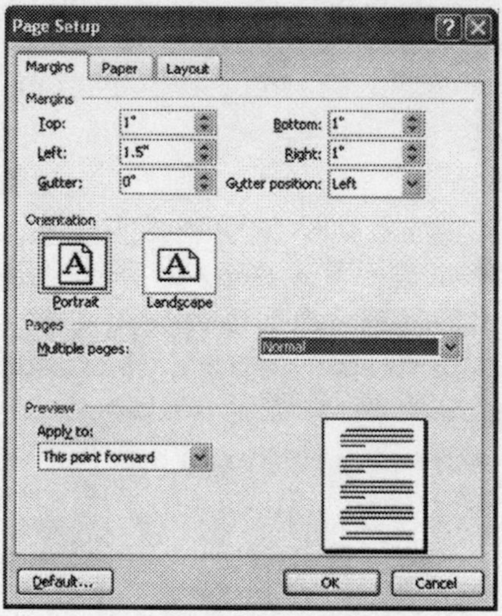

Figure 2-16

When you print out your document, your facing page will be printed with the correct mirror layout. Be sure to physically turn the page over, so the printed side is facing to the rear, before submitting the dissertation for binding.

2.10 Saving your chapter

When you've completed creating your chapter, you must save it. Go to the **File** menu and select **Save As** (see Figure 2-17). In the **Save As** dialog box, type a name for the file (let's call it **Chapter 1**), and from the **Save as type** pull-down menu, select **Word Document (*.doc)**. Using the **Save In** box, navigate to the location where you are saving your dissertation files. Click on **Save**.

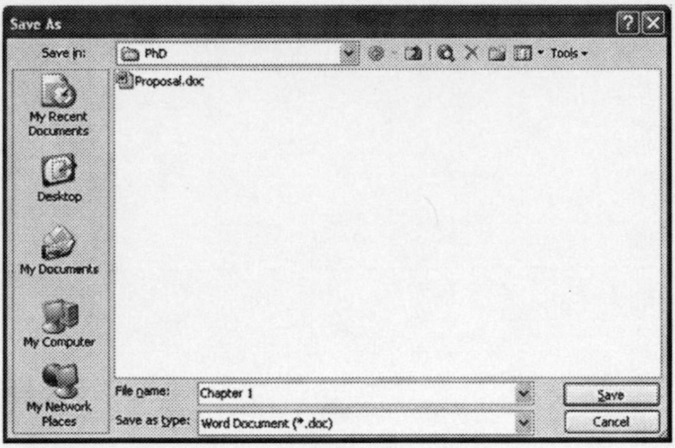

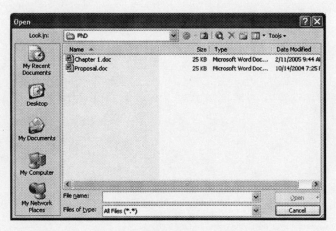

Figure 2-17

2.11 Revising your chapter

To revise your chapter, click on **File** and then on **Open.** Using the
Look in box, navigate to the folder that contains your dissertation files.
Click on **Chapter 1,** assuming that's the name you gave it (Figure 2-18).
After making any revisions, be sure to save the revised file, following the
instructions in section 1.8.

Figure 2-18

Chapter 3

Tables

Tables are a wonderfully efficient way of presenting certain kinds of information to the reader. Tables allow information to be arranged in categories, which helps the reader see broad patterns and make comparisons. Also, by providing a place for details (particularly numerical details) outside of the main text, tables can help the adept author avoid turgid prose. As a result, it is no surprise that many dissertations are laden with tables.

Word 2003 offers powerful capabilities for creating, formatting, and manipulating tables—often with more than one way to achieve a desired effect. In this chapter, we work through the basics of creating tables, using the features that are most commonly required in theses and dissertations.

3.1 Plan your table

Once you get deep into the formatting of a table, it can be a real hassle to modify it—say, if you discover that you forgot a column. So, before you pick up your mouse to create the table, think through how you want to present your data. Every table, however simple, has certain elements:

1. *Title.* A simple description of the table.
2. *Headings* (also called *heads*). The titles above the data in the table. A heading that appears above a single column of data is

called a *column heading*; every column in a table must have a column heading. A heading that runs across the top of more than one column of data is termed a *column spanner.*

3. *Stubs.* The text that appears in the leftmost column of the table.
4. *Stubheads.* The heading for the stubs.
5. *The body.* The rows and columns of data in your table. Each entry in the body is called a *cell.*
6. Many tables also include *notes* after the body. These notes may include explanations, explanations of statistical abbreviations in the text, or even citations of the sources of data reported in the table.
7. Some tables are broken into sections, each of which reports information on subgroups, using *table spanners,* or headings that run across the entire width of the table. For example, a table might first report results for men and then for women; the first section of the table would start with a table spanner labeled "Men" and the second section would start with a table spanner labeled "Women."

Many style manuals present general guidance for constructing tables, and you should consult yours to determine what information you need to include and any special formatting requirements. Another great resource for designing tables for a dissertation is *Presenting Your Findings: A Practical Guide for Creating Tables,* by Adelheid A. M. Nicol and Penny M. Pexman (1999, American Psychological Association), which discusses many statistical and nonstatistical tables that are often used in scholarly writing.

Now sketch out a design for your tables, on paper. Include all headings and stubs. If you are going to have more than one line of headings, show each. If you will use column spanners, be sure to determine how many columns each column spanner will cover. If you are going to have more than one line of headings, show each of them. Sketch out how many lines of data you plan to have in the table, and if you plan to break up the data with table spanners, show these too. If the table needs to be accompanied by any notes, include a row for them at the bottom of the table. By looking at your sketch, you can count up the total number of columns and rows that you will need.

3.2   Creating the table

Put your cursor at the point in your document where you want the table to appear. If you want the table to start on a new page, click on **Insert** and then **Break** and then make sure that the **Page break** radio button is checked; then click **OK**. However, many dissertation style manuals require that a table appear in the body of the text soon after the table is first mentioned; in such a case, you may want to insert your table immediately after the first paragraph that mentions it. Or your university may permit tables to be gathered together at the end of the dissertation.

To create the table, click on **Table** and then **Insert** and then **Table**. The **Insert Table** dialog box will come up (Figure 3-1). Fill in the number of columns and rows that you determined when you sketched out your table. Under **AutoFit behavior**, pick either **Fixed column width** or **AutoFit to contents**. The first choice will automatically create a table that is as wide as is allowed by your page margins, and each column will be of equal width; despite the option's name, each column's width can be changed later. The second option will create a table whose column widths will be automatically changed in order to accommodate the data in the table, so a column containing only single digits will be made narrower than another column that contains lengthy words. (Do not choose the third option, **AutoFit to window**. This is intended for designing tables that will be viewed in Web browsers.)

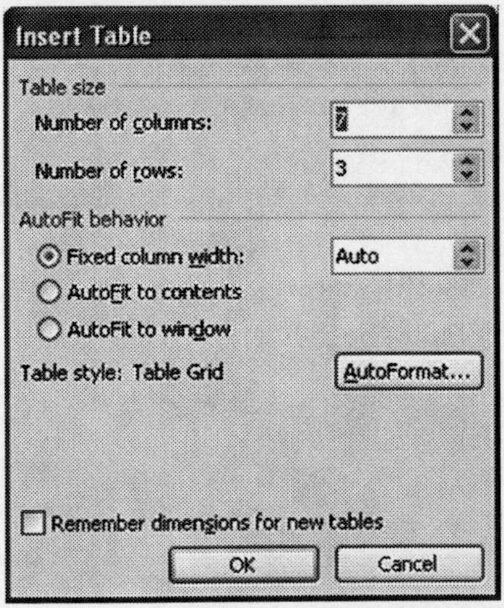

Figure 3-1

Unless you have customized your table styles, the dialog box will show the **Table style** as **Table Grid**. This is a useful style for the early stages of creating a table, so leave this unchanged.

If the dialog box lists a table style other than **Table Grid**, click on the **AutoFormat** button and scroll through the list of styles to find **Table Grid** (Figure 3-2). Highlight it and click on the **OK** button to get back to the **Insert Table** dialog box.

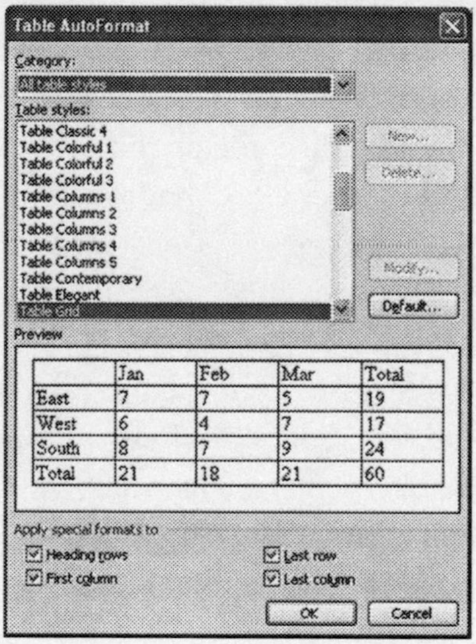

Figure 3-2

If you expect other tables in your document to have the same number of rows and columns (unlikely, but it does happen), check the box for **Remember dimensions for new tables**. When you next insert a table, Word 2003 will use the same settings.

Click **OK** when you are done setting the dimensions for your table, and Word 2003 will insert a blank table into your document. Don't worry yet if there are some horizontal or vertical rules that you want to erase; we will take care of that later.

3.2.1   Table placement

You can control the horizontal placement of your table on the page: Click once in the table and then click on **Table** and then **Table**

Properties to get the **Table Properties** dialog box. Click on the **Table** tab (Figure 3-3). In the **Alignment** section, you can determine whether the table should be aligned along the left margin, centered, or aligned along the right margin. If you choose **Left**, you also can use the **Indent from left** box. You can set a distance, in inches, for the table to be indented from the left.

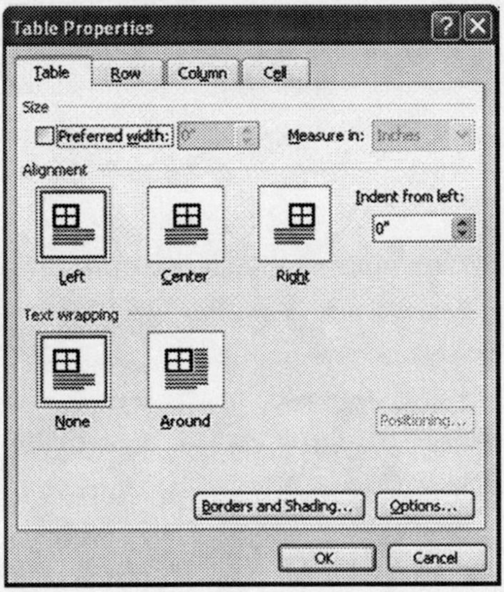

Figure 3-3

In the **Text wrapping** section, you can determine if Word 2003 should place body text on the right-hand side of the table if there is space to do so. Click **Around** if you want this or **None** if you do not. Click **OK**.

3.2.2   Add the headings

In filling out your table, first enter the column headings for your table. Put the cursor in each table cell that should have a heading and type the text that you want to appear. You can format the column heading by first highlighting it, then clicking on **Format** and **Font**, selecting the font, font size, style, and underlining that you want, and then clicking **OK**. (Note that some universities do permit tables to use different or smaller fonts than the dissertation's body text. This can be useful when trying to fit a large table onto a single page.) Or you can make the column headings left-aligned, right-aligned, or centered by highlighting them and then clicking on **Format** and **Paragraph** and choosing a selection in the **General** section in the **Alignment** drop-down menu.

If you used the **Fixed-column width** option for creating the table, you may find that text for the headings may be too wide or too narrow. Making a cell more or less wide is easy: Position your cursor over the cell border that you wish to move. When the cursor changes to a double-headed arrow, left-click with your mouse and drag the border to its desired position. As you drag, a vertical line will move along with the cursor; this signifies that you are moving the edge of an entire column and not just the border of one cell.

Create column spanners and table spanners by highlighting all the cells that the spanner should occupy. Then click on **Table** and then on **Merge Cells**. The cells will be melded into a single cell.

If you discover that you need to add an additional column, click in the column to the right of where you want the new column to go. Click on **Table** and then **Insert**, and then **Columns to the left**, and a new column will be added.

When you are done creating your columns headings or spanners, highlight all the rows that contain the headings. Then click **Table** and then **Heading Rows Repeat** (Figure 3-4). This instructs Word 2003 that the selected rows are headings. If the table does not fit on one page, Word 2003 will repeat the headings at the top of the continuation of the table on the second page. This is not visible when you view the document in **Normal** mode, but it does appear when you view the document in **Page Layout** mode (click on **View** and **Page Layout**) or in **Print Preview** (click on **File** and **Print Preview**).

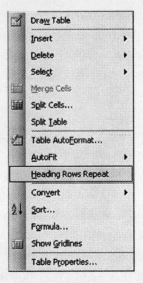

Figure 3-4

3.2.3   Add the table body

Next, enter the stubs and data to appear underneath the headings in the table. To move from one cell to another, you can use the arrow keys on your keyboard. Or use the **Tab** key to move to the next cell in a row and the **Shift** and **Tab** keys simultaneously to move to the previous cell in a row.

If you changed the font characteristics of your headings, you should also change them for your data, so that your table will have a consistent look. As with the heading text, you can format your table body by highlighting the cells, then clicking on **Format** and **Font**, selecting the font, font size, style, and underlining that you want, and clicking **OK.**

If you discover that your table needs more rows, position your cursor in the row above where you want the new row to appear. Click **Table,** then **Insert,** then **Rows below**, and a new row will be inserted.

3.2.4   Adjusting column widths

Frequently you will decide that you want to make a given column narrower or wider. You can easily do this by using your mouse to grab the table line that you want to move and then dragging it to the desired position.

3.2.5   Aligning the columns

Usually, you want the numbers in a table's vertical column to line up nicely. To format the alignment of data in a column, highlight the cells that you want to align. Then click on **Format** and then on **Paragraph**. In the **General** section, under **Alignment,** (Figure 3-5), you can select **Left**, **Centered**, **Right,** or **Justified** alignment. If you want **Left** or **Right** alignment, but also want the numbers indented a bit from the left or right edge of the cell, you can also set a nonzero value for **Left** or **Right** in the **Indentation** section of the dialog box. Click **OK.**

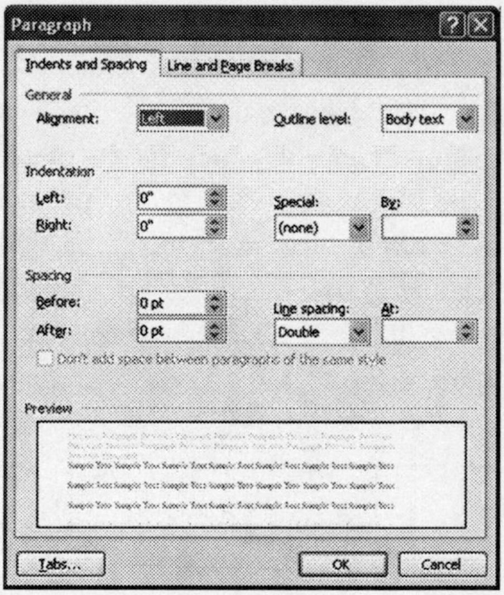

Figure 3-5

Often, you want a column of numbers to be lined up along the decimal point, but the numbers have a varying number of digits, so using **Left** or **Right** alignment doesn't create the right effect. In these cases, you can use **Decimal** alignment: Highlight the cells that you want to be decimal aligned. Then click on **Format** and then **Tabs**. The

Tabs dialog box will come up. Under **Alignment**, click the **Decimal** radio button, and under **Leader**, click the **None** radio button. Under **Tab stop position,** enter the distance, in inches, from the left edge of the cell where you would like the decimal point to appear (Figure 3-6). Click **Set** and then **OK**, and the data will be aligned. If you want to move the decimal alignment spot, highlight the cells again. With your cursor, grab the decimal alignment icon in the ruler (Figure 3-7) and drag it to the desired alignment spot; the data in the highlighted cells will be automatically realigned.

Figure 3-6

Figure 3-7

3.2.6   Add the table notes

Many tables include notes, such as explanatory material and statistical explanations. Although the notes appear separate from the table, it is helpful to construct your table so that the notes actually are included in the last row of the table; this will ensure that if you move the table to another point in your document, the notes will go with the table.

First, merge all the columns in the last row: Highlight the entire last row, and then click on **Table** and then **Merge Cells**. Then enter your note or notes into this last row.

Also, be sure that if you modified the font characteristics of your headings and table body, you do the same for the text in the table notes.

3.2.7 Getting the rules right

Now that the words and numbers are in your table, you can finalize the use of horizontal and vertical lines, or rules, in your table. Style manuals vary on this point. The *Publication Manual of the American Psychological Association*, for example, forbids the use of vertical rules, and calls for limited use of horizontal rules—specifically, lines separating the table title from the table headings, the table headings from the body of the text, and the body of the text from table notes. Turabian's *A Manual for Writers of Term Papers, Theses, and Dissertations* says that if rules are used, there should be one above the headings and one before the table notes.

By using the table gridline format when you created the table, Word 2003 has drawn every possible ruling in your table: every cell has a line on the top, bottom, left and right. Now you should erase the rulings that your style forbids you from having.

To do so, click on **View,** then **Toolbars,** and then **Tables and Borders**. On the **Tables and Borders** toolbar (Figure 3-8), left click once on the eraser icon (Figure 3-9). Your cursor will turn into the eraser icon. Move to the table. Place the cursor on a line that you want erased, press on your mouse's left button, and drag the cursor along that line while holding the left button. When you release the left button, the line or lines that you have highlighted will be erased. Vertical lines will disappear entirely; horizontal lines will be visible as grayed-out lines that will not print in the final document.

Figure 3-8

Figure 3-9

You also can change the width of the rulings that remain in the table. For example, you may want rulings within the body of your table to be thinner than the ones that Word 2003 uses by default. To change the width, click on **View** and then **Toolbars** and then **Tables and Borders**. From the **Line style** drop-down menu (Figure 3-10), pick the style of ruling that you desire (generally, the single, unbroken line may be best for dissertations). From the **Line Weight** drop-down menu immediately to its right on the toolbar, select the width, in points, for the line. Click on the **Border Color** button next to the width menu to select the color of the line (**Black** is generally best for dissertations). Now click on the **Draw Table** icon (Figure 3-11). Your cursor will turn into a pencil icon. Move to the table and place the icon on a line that you want changed, press on your mouse's left button, and drag the cursor along that line while holding the left button. When you release the left button, the line or lines that you have highlighted will be changed to the format specified in the **Tables and Borders** toolbar.

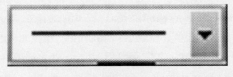

Figure 3-10

Figure 3-11

3.2.8 Using rules with column spanners

Most horizontal rules in a table stretch across the entire width of the table. But one exception is with column spanners. When two column spanners appear right next to each other on the same line of a table's headings, there should be a break in the horizontal rule between the two column spanners.

To create this break, use Word 2003 to draw a vertical white line through the horizontal black ruling at the point where you want the break to be. Click on **View,** then **Toolbars,** and then **Tables and Borders**. From the **Line Style** drop-down menu, pick the single, unbroken line. From the **Line Weight** drop-down menu, select a width of **6 points** (½ of an inch). Click on the **Border Color** button and then click on the color **White** from the color palette. Now click on the **Draw Table** icon (Figure 3-11). Your cursor will turn into a pencil icon. Move to the table and place the icon on the cell boundary where you want the break in the horizontal line to appear. Press on your mouse's left button and drag the cursor down through the horizontal black line (do not stop at the black line; you must drag through it) while holding the left button. When you release the left button, a white line will be created that will cut through the horizontal black ruling.

3.3　Adding a title

Most dissertation style manuals require that each table have a title, even if the dissertation has only one table. These are better produced in Word 2003, even if you paste your table from another source (section 3.8), so that you can be sure that the table titles adhere to your university's formatting requirements and are consistent with the rest of the dissertation. Moreover, if you use Word 2003's table titling capabilities, you will have an easier time when you must create a list of tables (section 7.4).

One confusing aspect of Word 2003 is that to create a table title, you actually use the program's facilities for figure captions. Click once anywhere within the table for which you would like to add a title. Then click on **Insert, Reference,** and then **Caption**. The **Caption** dialog box will come up (Figure 3-12). From the **Label** drop-down menu, make sure that **Table** is selected; if it is, the **Caption** box will contain the text **"Table"** followed by a number. From the **Position** drop-down menu, pick the location that your dissertation style manual prescribes for table titles; in most cases, you should choose **Above selected item**.

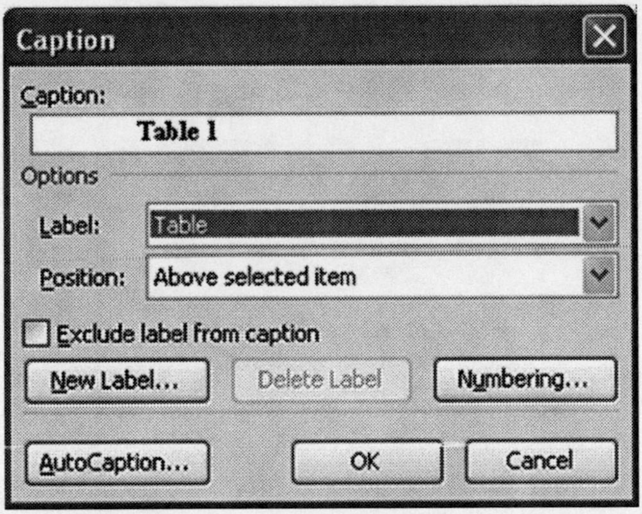

Figure 3-12

Then in the **Caption** box, type the title for the table. (You may want to add a period or other punctuation after the figure number.) Then click **OK**, and the title will be added above the table.

Some style manuals, such as the American Psychological Association's, require that the table title occupy two lines: on the first is the table label and number, and on the second is the descriptive title. To enter a two-line title, type it all in the **Caption** box, but press **Shift** and **Enter** simultaneously where you want the line break to occur.

In the **Caption** box, you cannot add special formatting to the title (such as italics or boldface). Rather, to change the formatting of a portion of your table title, wait until you have clicked **OK** and the title has been deposited in your dissertation text. Then you can reformat some or all of the title as you wish, and you can add special characters as well (section 2.7).

3.4   Page breaks

Some tables are too long to fit on a single page. Word 2003 will automatically split a row where it thinks best. However, you can stop this behavior: Position your cursor in the row that you do not want broken across pages. Then click on **Table** and **Table Properties** and then the

Row tab (Figure 3-13). Uncheck the box **Allow row to break across pages** and then click **OK**.

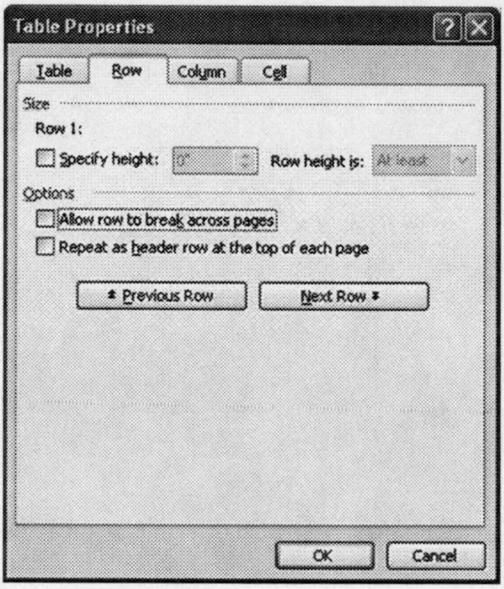

Figure 3-13

Now you should tell Word 2003 where you want the page breaks to appear in your table. Place your cursor in the row that you want to be the first on the new page. Then press the **Ctrl** and **Enter keys** simultaneously, or click on **Insert** and **Break** and then **Page break** and finally on **OK**. However, one drawback of Word 2003 is that when you manually insert a page break in this manner, Word 2003 does not repeat column headings at the top of the new page, even if you have designated the headings on your table for it to do so (section 3.2.2). If you wish to have Word 2003 repeat the column headings (and you probably should do so), you may wish to use this alternative approach to trick Word 2003 into creating the page break where you want it: Find the row that you want to be the last row on the page. Float your cursor over the bottom edge of that row until it becomes the resize pointer (Figure 3-14). Left-click on the row border and drag the border toward the bottom of the page until the row beneath it is automatically pushed onto the next page.

Figure 3-14

If a table continues onto a second page, you may need to add a horizontal rule at the bottom of the first page; check your style manual. Follow the directions in section 3.2.7 for adding the rules.

3.5   Landscape tables

In most dissertations, all pages are printed in the portrait orientation—that is, with the long edge of the paper running vertically. However, if your dissertation includes tables that are very wide, you may need to place those tables on landscape pages, with the long edge of the paper running horizontally.

Word 2003 handles landscaped tables without a problem. But it does have a problem with landscaped pages in general: Page numbers are put in the wrong place (at least in the eyes of most dissertation style manuals), and Word 2003 does not offer an easy way to reposition the page numbers. So we offer this workaround: Delete page numbers from landscaped pages and add them back (sort of) when the pages are printed.

3.5.1   Creating a new section for the landscape page

First, you must create a new section in your Word file for the landscape page. Place your cursor at the point where you want the landscape table to appear. Then click **Insert** and then **Break**. In the **Section breaks** section of the dialog box, click on **Next page**. Click **OK**.

Then repeat the steps in the previous paragraph one more time, to create another new section in which the dissertation will return to portrait orientation for the material that follows the landscape table. This procedure creates two section breaks—one for when your dissertation goes from portrait to landscape orientation, and a second for reverting back to portrait orientation.

3.5.2   *Deleting the landscape page number*

Now we will alter Word's handling of page numbers. Your cursor now is in the second portrait section—that is, the one that will follow the landscape page. Usually, Word assumes that page numbers in one section of a Word file are handled the same as page numbers in the previous section. You must adjust this behavior because of the landscape page.

Click on **View** and then on **Header and Footer**. Word 2003 will display the header and footer for the portrait section, surrounded by dashed lines and labeled **Header -Section X-** and **Footer -Section X-** (where X is a number), along with the **Header and Footer** toolbar (Figure 3-15). Click once in the header or footer—whichever contains the page number. On the toolbar, click on the **Link to Previous** button (Figure 3-16) to tell Word 2003 that the header and footer in this portrait section should not be the same as the landscape section that precedes it.

Figure 3-15

Figure 3-16

Now move to the landscape section by clicking on the **Show Previous** button (Figure 3-17). You will see the header or footer for the landscape section. There too, click on the **Link to Previous** button to instruct Word that page numbers in the landscape section will be treated differently than page numbers in the portrait section that comes before it.

Figure 3-17

Use your cursor to highlight the page number in the header of the landscape section. Click on the **Delete** key to eliminate the page number. Click **Close** on the **Header and Footer** toolbar.

Then change this section to landscape orientation: Click on **File**, then on **Page Setup**, and then on the **Margins** tab. From the **Apply to** drop-down menu, pick **This section**. Under **Orientation**, click on the **Landscape** icon; the margins will automatically adjust themselves accordingly (Figure 3-18). Click on **OK**.

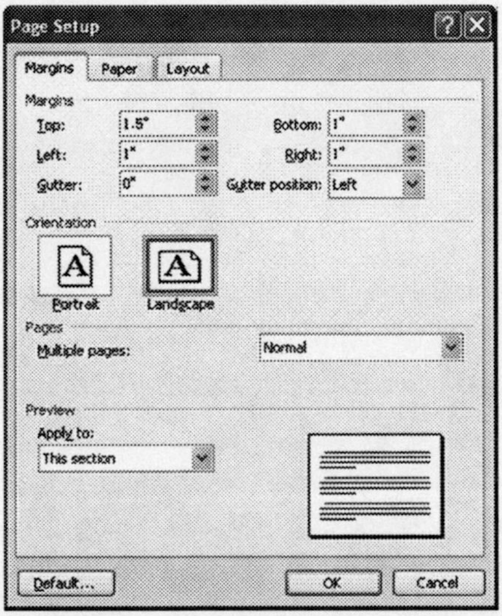

Figure 3-18

Now insert your table in the landscape section. If the table requires more than one page, Word 2003 will automatically add the additional pages that are necessary.

If another landscape table follows immediately after this landscape table, you can add it right after the first landscape table. If you wish to create a page break between the two tables, click **Insert** and **Break** and **Page break** and **OK** immediately after the first table.

After you are finished with the landscape section, click in the section that you added after the landscape section and resume work in portrait orientation.

3.6   Copying a table

You may want to copy a table. Put your cursor in the table that you want to copy. Click on **Table** and then **Select** and then **Table**. This selects the entire table. Click on **Edit** and then **Copy**, to copy the table to the clipboard. Now put your cursor where you want the copy to appear. Click on **Edit** and then **Paste**. Note that the title will not be copied along with the table, so you will have to title the copy (section 3.3).

3.7   Deleting a table

If you decide that you no longer want a table in your document, getting rid of it is also easy. Put your cursor anywhere in the table. Click on **Table,** then **Select,** and then **Table**. This selects the entire table. Click again on **Table,** then on **Delete,** and then on **Rows**. This deletes the selected table. If you have given the table a title, you must delete the title manually.

If you want to keep the table but delete its contents, highlight the cells that you want to empty. (Or if you want to empty the entire table, click in the table and then click on **Table, Select,** and then **Table**.) Press the **Delete** key.

3.8   Consider: Is there another way?

Before you plunge into the task of using Word 2003 to create the tables in your dissertation, consider whether there are other, easier ways of getting the job done. Word 2003 is incredibly powerful, but many people find its tables features a bit daunting and confusing. But if you can create your tables in another Windows program, you can then import them into your Word 2003 dissertation—and you may save yourself considerable time and effort.

For example, if your tables will report statistical information that is being generated by statistical software, check if that software can create tables in the format that you need. Many statistical programs offer options for customizing tables. If your statistical program offers a suitable format, you could paste a copy of the tables it produces into your Word 2003 document (see section 3.8.2).

Or you could consider entering your table into a spreadsheet program such as Microsoft Excel, formatting it as you desire, and then pasting the table into Word 2003. Although many people think that spreadsheets contain only numbers, today's spreadsheet programs can handle text just as well as numbers, so this approach works for word tables as well as for numerical tables.

Caution: Whichever approach you use, be sure to follow your institution's formatting rules for fonts, line spacing, and table rules. In most cases, it is easier to make sure that these formats are correct in the first place than to try to revise them after the table has been imported into Word 2003.

3.8.1 Inserting table from a file

If you saved your table as a file (such as a Microsoft Excel spreadsheet), go into Word 2003 and be sure your cursor is positioned where you want the table to appear. Then click on **Insert**, then on **Object**, and then on the **Create from File** tab (Figure 3-19). Check the **Link to file** box if you want Word 2003 to automatically update the table if you modify the table in the program that created it. Be sure that the **Display as icon** box is *not* checked.

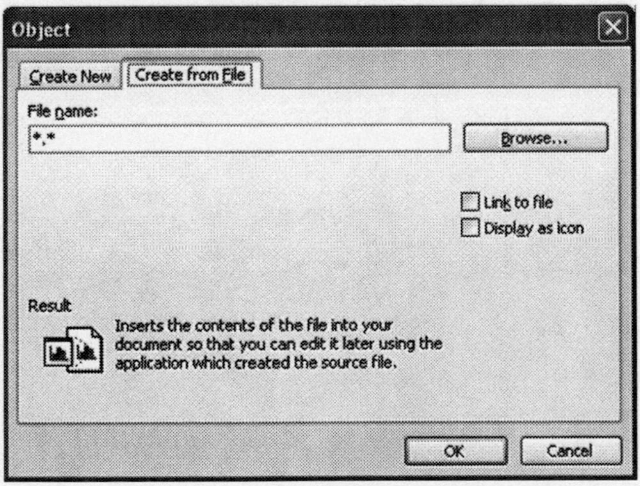

Figure 3-19

Use the **Browse** button to navigate to the file that contains the table. Click **Insert,** then **OK,** and the table will be inserted into your file. To edit it using the original program, click twice anywhere within the table. Add a title to the table by clicking on the table and then clicking on **Insert** and **Reference** and **Caption** (section 3.3).

3.8.2   *Copying a table from another program*

Alternatively, if you are using another program to create the table, you can copy it to the Windows clipboard (usually by selecting the table and then using the **Copy** command in the program that is generating the image). You also can often select only part of the table—such as specific rows from an Excel spreadsheet—and copy that portion to the clipboard.

Then place your cursor in the blank paragraph in your dissertation where you want the image to appear (see section 4.1). Click on **Edit** and then on **Paste**.) A copy of the table will be inserted into your file. Add a title to the table by clicking on the table and then clicking on **Insert, Reference,** and **Caption** (section 3.3).

Chapter 4

Using figures

I n dissertations, the term "figure" generally refers to charts, graphs, images, and other nontextual material (and it does not include tables, which we treat separately in Chapter 3). Examples of figures could include photographs that you have scanned into a digital format, a histogram produced by statistical software, and an organizational chart that you produced with a graphics program (or even the graphics capabilities of Word 2003). Word 2003 provides many ways that you can create and manipulate graphics and insert them into word-processing documents; the options can be bewildering for the novice user of Word 2003. Fortunately, most graduate schools demand simplicity in the use of graphics in dissertations, so many of Word 2003's capabilities can be ignored. In this chapter, we present a step-by-step process for inserting graphics into your dissertation.

Note: In general, it is wise to avoid using color in graphics in a dissertation. Most dissertations are microfilmed in black and white, in which colors in the original dissertation are lost. If possible, even avoid varying shades of gray, because these may be difficult to distinguish in the microfilmed copy. The best option is to use a variety of crosshatching.

4.1 Find the spot

Before you insert an image into your dissertation, first identify which paragraph in your document should immediately precede the chart.

(Many dissertation style manuals require that figures appear in the text shortly after they are first mentioned in the text. Some style manuals also permit figures to be gathered together at the end of each chapter.) Place your cursor at the end of the paragraph that is to come immediately before your graphic.

Then create a blank paragraph by hitting **Enter**. Eliminate any indentation for this single paragraph *only*, by clicking on **Format,** then **Paragraph**, and then the **Indents and Spacing** tab. In the **Indentation** section, select **(none)** from the **Special** drop-down menu. If you are using Word's **Exactly** setting for line spacing in the **Line Spacing** drop-down menu in the **Spacing** section, you also must disable that setting for the image by selecting **Single** (Figure 4-1). Click on **OK** to close the dialog box and to return to your blank paragraph.

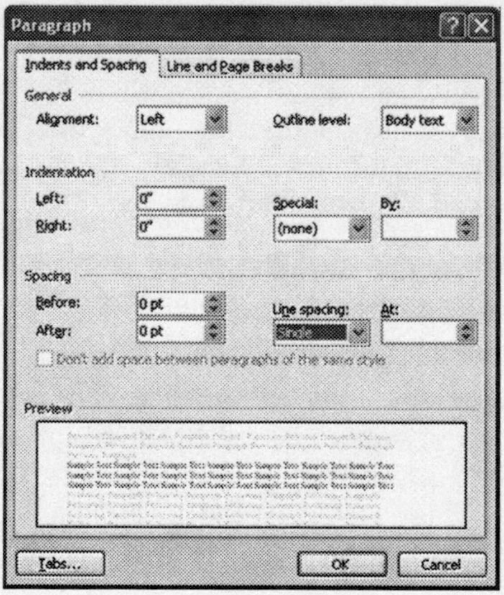

Figure 4-1

4.2   Inserting an image from a file

It is generally easiest if you save each image to be used in your dissertation in a separate file. Word 2003 can read a wide variety of graphics formats, including .bmp, .dib, .gif, .jpg, .pcx, .png, .tif, .wmf, .tga, and .pcd files. Creating the graphics separately eliminates the risk that a mis-step on your part could inadvertently wreck some part of your dissertation text.

If you are inserting an entire image from a file, go into Word 2003 and be sure your cursor is positioned in the blank paragraph where your image will reside (see previous section). Then click on **Insert**, then on **Picture**, and then on **From File**. Navigate to the location of your image file (Figure 4-2). Click the **Insert** button, and a copy of the image will be inserted into your Word 2003 file.

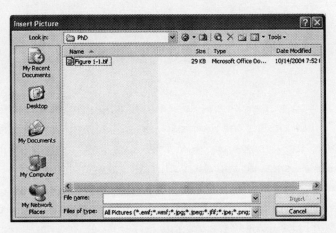

Figure 4-2

4.2.1   Positioning the image

Next, you need to give Word some directions about the graphic. First, instruct Word not to try to put text to the left or right of the figure: Click on the graphic and then click on **Format** and **Picture** and the **Layout** tab (Figure 4-3). Under **Wrapping style,** click on **Square.** Next, tell Word about the graphic's position: Under **Horizontal alignment,** click **Center** if you want the graphic centered between the left and right margins or **Left** if you want it aligned with the left-hand margin. Click **OK.**

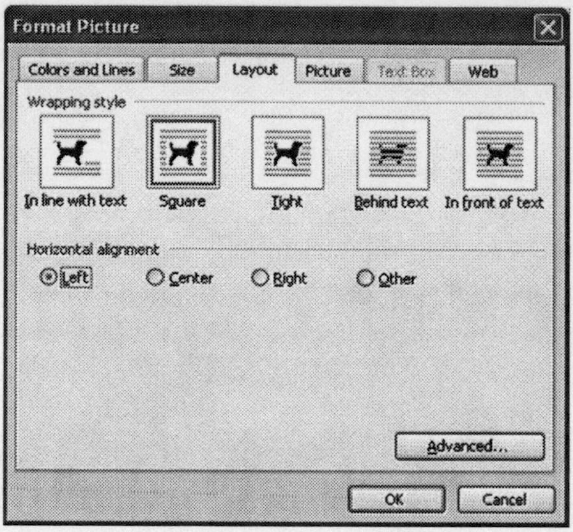

Figure 4-3

Now you can move the image in the file by left-clicking on the graphic and moving the mouse, while still holding the left button, to drag it to the desired location. For more precise positioning, click once on the graphic and then click on **Format** and **Picture** and the **Layout** tab (Figure 4-3). Then click on the **Advanced** button. The **Picture Position** tab provides options for specifying the vertical and horizontal positions of the graphic (Figure 4-4). You can specify them in inches in the **Absolute position** boxes, or you can order the graphic to be aligned along the left or right margins or page boundaries, or centered horizontally or vertically. Click **OK** twice when you are done, and your graphic will be repositioned.

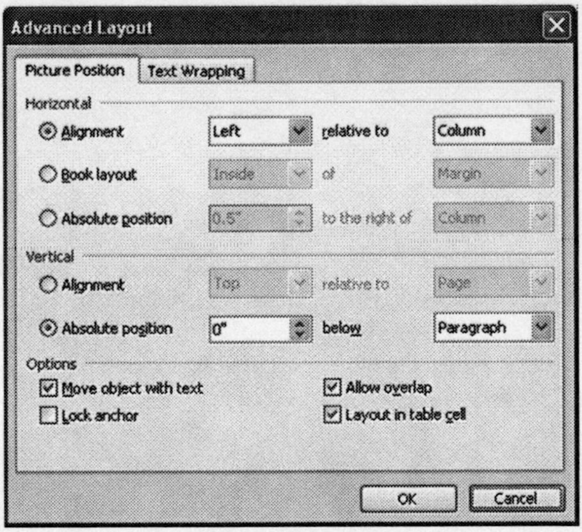

Figure 4-4

4.2.2   Resizing the image

You also can enlarge or reduce the image's size by using your mouse to grab any of the corners of the image and dragging it to make the image larger or smaller. When a corner is dragged in this fashion, Word 2003 changes the image's horizontal and vertical dimensions simultaneously, keeping them in the right proportions. Or to do the enlargement or reduction with more precision, click once on the graphic and then click on **Format** and **Picture** and the **Size** tab (see Figure 4-5). Be sure that the button **Lock aspect ratio** is checked. You can enter any desired value for height, and Word 2003 will automatically compute the proportional width, or vice versa. Click **OK** when done.

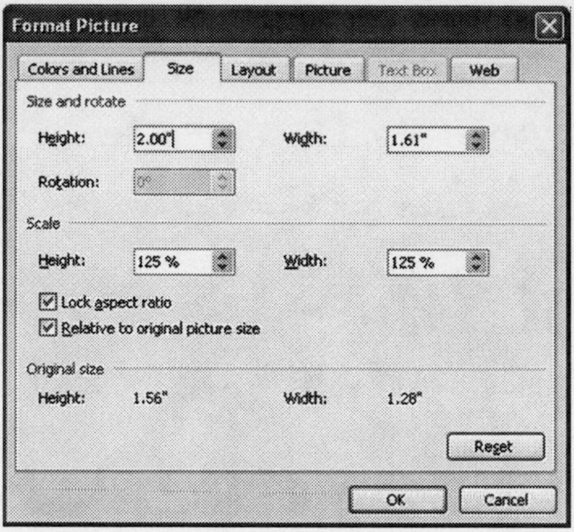

Figure 4-5

4.3   Copying an image from another program

Alternatively, if you are using another program to create the image, you can copy the image to the Windows clipboard (usually by using the **Copy** command in the program that is generating the image). You also can often select only part of the image—such as specified rows from an Excel spreadsheet—and copy that portion to the clipboard.

Then place your cursor in the blank paragraph in your dissertation where you want the image to appear (see section 4.1).

Click on **Edit**, and then on **Paste Special**. In the **Paste Special** dialog box (Figure 4-6), be sure that the **Paste** radio button is checked. From the **As** menu in the dialog box, click once on the format in which you want the image to be inserted into your text—usually **Picture (Windows Metafile)** and **Picture (Enhanced Metafile),** if available, are good choices if you plan to make the graphic larger or smaller. Bitmap and Device Independent Bitmap are good choices for a graphic that will appear in your dissertation at its original size; a graphic in either format may suffer some degradation when it is made larger or smaller. Click **OK**, and a copy of the image will be inserted into your file.

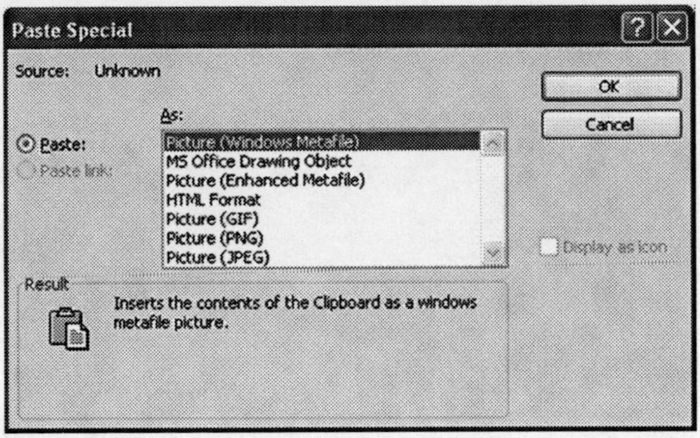

Figure 4-6

You can reposition the image (section 4.2.1) or change its size (section 4.2.2).

4.4   Figure captions

Most dissertation style manuals require that each figure have a caption. These are better produced in Word 2003 rather than in any other program that you might have used to create the figures themselves, so that you can be sure that the figure captions adhere to your university's formatting requirements and are consistent with the rest of the dissertation. Moreover, if you use Word 2003's captioning capabilities, you will have an easier time when you create a table of figures (section 7.4).

Select the image for which you would like to add a caption by clicking on it once. Then click on **Insert** and then **Reference** and then **Caption**. The **Caption** dialog box will come up (Figure 4-7). Make sure **Exclude label from caption** is not checked. From the **Label** drop-down menu, make sure that Figure is selected; if it is, the **Caption** box will have the word "Figure" followed by a number. From the **Position** drop-down menu, pick the location that your dissertation style manual prescribes for figure captions; in most cases, you should choose **Below selected item**.

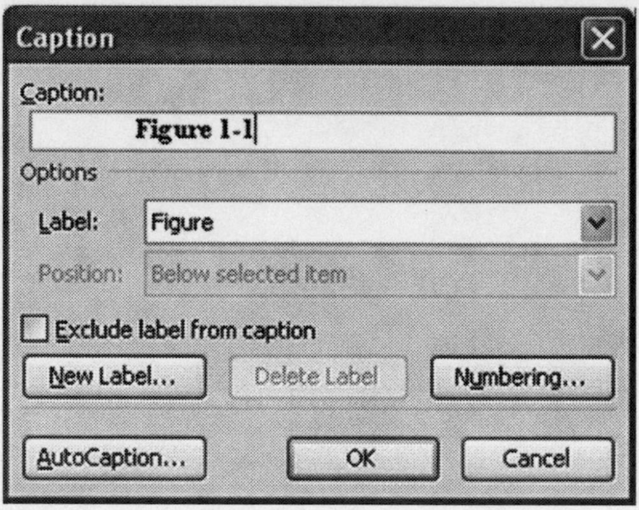

Figure 4-7

Then in the **Caption** box, type the remainder of your caption. (You may want to add a period or other punctuation after the figure number.) Then click **OK**, and the caption will be added to your text.

You may want your figure caption to occupy two lines, with the figure label and number on the first line and the descriptive title on the second. To enter a two-line caption, type it all in the **Caption** box, click **OK**, and then in the caption as it appears on your text press **Shift** and **Return** simultaneously where you want the line break to occur.

You cannot add special formatting to the text (such as italics or bold-face) in the **Caption** box. To change the formatting of a portion of your caption text, wait until you have clicked **OK** and the caption has been deposited in your dissertation text. Then you can reformat some or all of the caption as you wish, and you can add special characters as well (section 2.7).

4.5 Landscape figures

In most dissertations, all figures appear in the portrait orientation—that is, with the top of the figure pointing vertically along the page. However, you may need to position one or more figures in landscape ori-entation, with the top of the figure pointing horizontally. You can do this without the hassle of creating whole landscape pages (section 3.5) by using Word 2003's abilities to rotate a figure on an ordinary portrait page by 90 degrees.

Place your cursor at the point where you want the figure to appear. Then click **Insert** and then **Break** and then **Page break** or (**Ctrl** plus **Enter**). Insert the figure onto the new page, following the directions in sections 4.2 or 4.3, depending on whether the image is in a separate file.

Next, highlight the picture by clicking on it once. Click on **Format** and then **Picture**. On the **Format Picture** dialog box, click on the **Layout** tab (Figure 4-3). In the **Wrapping Style** section, click once on **Square**; the setting for **Horizontal alignment** doesn't matter because you are going to change its horizontal alignment in a moment. Click on **OK**.

Now move the graphic roughly to the middle of the page by clicking on it and dragging it with your mouse.

If the **Drawing** toolbar is not visible, show it by clicking on **View** and **Toolbars** and **Drawing**. Make sure the figure is still selected. On the toolbar, click on the **Draw** button and then **Rotate or Flip** and **Rotate Left 90°**. This will rotate the image 90 degrees to the left, getting it into landscape orientation.

Once the image is rotated, move it to its final location on the page (section 4.2.1). If necessary, you can enlarge or reduce the image's size so that it remains within the page's margins (section 4.2.2).

Now add a figure caption, following the instructions in section 4.4. Word 2003 will create the caption as if the figure were in portrait orientation—that is, the caption will run horizontally across the page. We'll correct this in a moment.

First, you must convert the caption from one using a Word 2003 construction called a "text box" to one using a Word 2003 construction called a "frame." The technical differences between the two don't matter except that a figure caption in a text box won't show up in your table of figures (section 7.4), while a caption in a frame will. Click once within the caption text to make the text box visible. Click once on the text box's border. Then click on **Format** and **Text Box.** In the **Format Text Box** dialog box, click **Text Box** and then the **Convert to Frame** button (Figure 4-8). You will get a confirmation dialog box (Figure 4-9). Click **OK**, and the caption will now be enclosed in a frame.

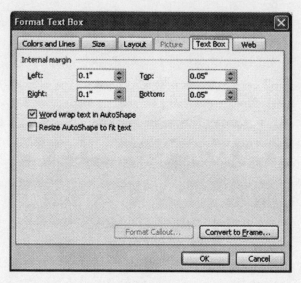

Figure 4-8

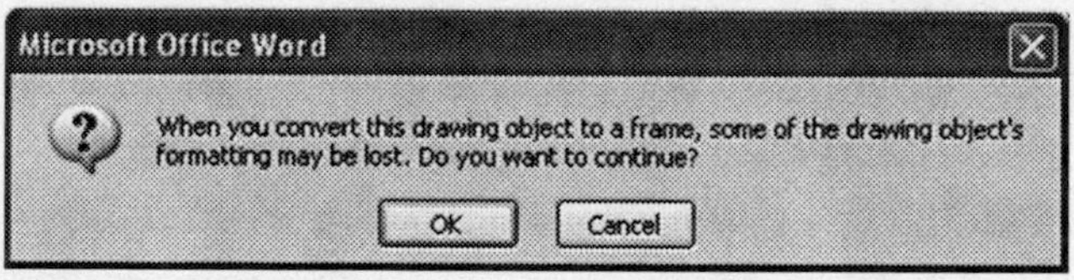

Figure 4-9

Now it's time to correctly position the caption text itself. Use your mouse to drag one of the frame's bottom corners to make it big enough for the caption text after it's been rotated. (Check your university's style manual. You may need to make the caption extend from the page's top margin to the bottom margin, so be sure to size the box properly.) Then click on **Format** and **Text direction** to get the **Text Direction-Text Frame** dialog box (Figure 4-10). Click on the icon that shows the text pointing to the left, and then click **OK**. The text will be rotated into landscape orientation. Finally, left-click on the edge of the frame and, while holding down the mouse button, drag the frame into the proper location. The text will move with it.

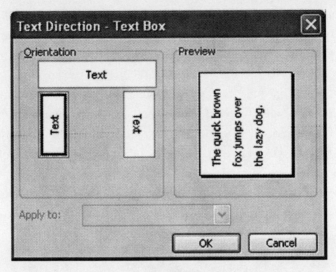

Figure 4-10

4.6   Figures as another approach to tables

It's worth noting that although Word 2003 can produce tables (as we saw in Chapter 3), you can instead apply the methodology described in this chapter to insert tables into your dissertation. In some cases, this may be easier and quicker. For example, if you are using a statistical analysis program that can generate data tables in the format that is required for your dissertation, and if the statistical analysis program allows you to paste those tables to the Windows clipboard or save them as stand-alone graphics files, you could paste or insert those tables into your document just as you would add any other figure.

If you take this approach, just remember that many universities require that table titles go above a table and figure captions go below a figure. So when you add the title for your pasted-in table (section 3.3), select **Above selected item** from the **Position** drop-down menu on the **Caption** dialog box (click **Insert**, **Reference**, and **Caption**).

4.7   Specialized figure types

Your dissertation may have one or more special categories of figures that you would like to give a common label. For example, you may have several maps, all of which you would rather be captioned as Map 1, Map 2, and so on rather than as Figure 1, Figure 2, and so on. Word 2003 makes it easy to create such customized categories of figures. In this example, we will use the category "Map," although you could well use "Illustration" or "Plate," or "Diagram."

Insert your first map into your dissertation as you would any other figure. However, when you click on **Insert** and **Reference** and **Caption** to add the figure caption (section 4.4), click on **New Label** to get the **New Label** dialog box (Figure 4-11). Enter the label for the new category of figures—in this example, that would be "Map." Click on **OK**. The **Caption** dialog box will be automatically revised to use **Map** as its label. Proceed as normally with finishing the caption.

Figure 4-11

When you add the second or additional maps to the dissertation and you are inserting the caption, select **Map** from the **Label** drop-down menu in the **Caption** dialog box.

4.8   Compressing figures

Images can take a lot of file space, and if your dissertation contains many images, it can balloon in size. But images often are larger than they need to be because they contain details too fine to reproduce on a laser printer. Word 2003 offers a way to compress images to remove details that will be invisible on your printed output.

Note: Unlike many editing changes in Word 2003, you cannot undo the compression process. Therefore, you might want to make a copy of your dissertation before compressing the images, in case you decide that you don't want to compress them after all.

To compress the images in your document, select any image by clicking once on it. Then click on **Format** and **Picture** to get the **Format Picture** dialog box (Figure 4-12). Click the **Compress** button to get the **Compress Pictures** dialog box (Figure 4-13). In the **Apply to** section, click the **Selected pictures** radio button if you only want the selected picture to be compressed, or click the **All pictures in document** radio button if you want all images compressed. In the **Change resolution** section, click the **Print** radio button. Under **Options**, check the **Compress pictures** box to use JPEG compression to the images, which may compress them further but may also degrade their quality somewhat. Check the **Delete cropped areas of pictures box** if you have cropped any of your images so that parts are invisible in the document and if you want those cropped portions permanently discarded (you will no longer be able to uncrop the images). Click **OK,** then **Apply,** and then **OK** once again.

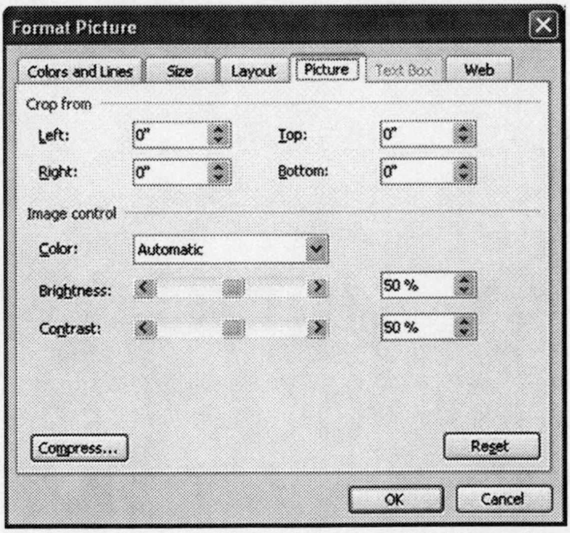

Figure 4-12

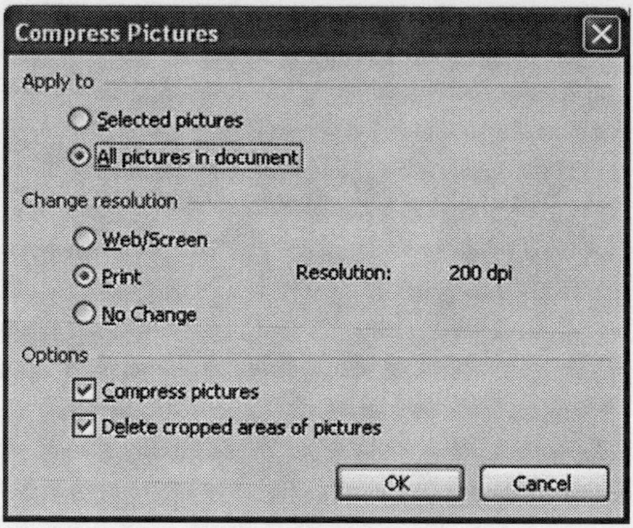
Compress Pictures
Apply to
Selected pictures
All pictures in document
Change resolution
Web/Screen
Print
Resolution:
200 dpi
No Change
Options
Compress pictures
Delete cropped areas of pictures
OK
Cancel

Figure 4-13

Chapter 5

Equations and formulas

M any dissertations include mathematical equations and formulas, which offer special challenges in word processing, because they often include special characters (such as symbols and Greek letters) and superscripts and subscripts, and can occupy more than one line of text. Word 2003 offers two separate techniques for entering and manipulating equations and formulas—one better suited to simple tasks, the other better suited to more complex equations and formulas.

5.1   Simple equations

If your equations and formulas are simple, and if you do not want to set them off from the text with a title/caption and number like figures and tables, then simply enter the equation or formula like any other text.

You can insert many special characters that are not available on your keyboard using Word's **Insert** command or by typing special Windows codes for the symbols (see section 2.7).

You also can add superscripts and subscripts to your formulas (like the 2's in $E = mc^2$ and H_2O). First, type the superscripts and subscripts as normal text: **H2O**, for example. Then there are two approaches for converting the normal text to superscripts or subscripts:

1.   Highlight the text that you want to be a superscript or a subscript.

Click on **Format** and **Font** and then on the **Font** tab. Check the **Superscript** box if you want the highlighted text to be a superscript or check the **Subscript** box if you want the text to be a subscript. Click **OK**. Figure 5-1 depicts how to do this for the 2 in H_2O.

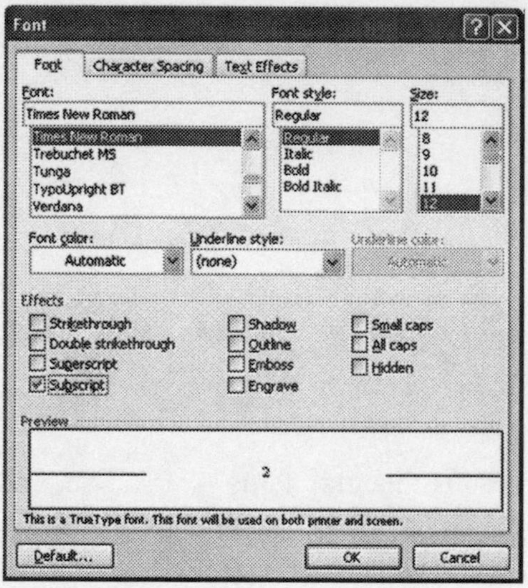

Figure 5-1

2. However, Word 2003 uses a small typeface for superscripts and subscripts, and some universities disapprove of this small typeface, out of concern that the superscripts and subscripts will be unclear in microfilmed versions of the dissertation. To avoid using the small typefaces, highlight the text that you want to be a superscript or subscript and click on **Format** and **Font** and the **Font** tab. Be sure the **Superscript** and **Subscript** boxes are *not* checked. Choose the font style and font size that you want for your superscript or subscript. Do *not* click **OK**. Rather, click on the **Character Spacing** tab. From the **Position** drop-down menu, pick **Raised** if you want a superscript or **Lowered** if you want a subscript. In the **By** field, enter the number of points that you would like the number to be above or below the text. (A reasonable value is half the

point size of your body type: that is, 5 if you are using 10-point type and 6 if you are using 12-point type.) Figure 5-2 shows how to do this for the 2 in H_2O. Click **OK.**

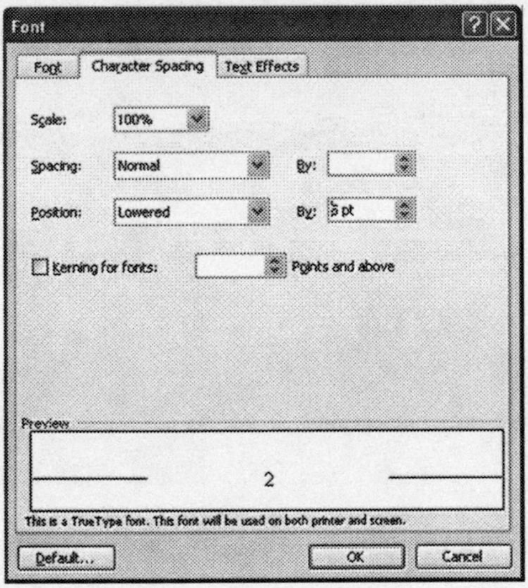

Figure 5-2

Note: If you use the second approach, in which you tweak the **Character Spacing** settings, you should use an **Exactly** setting for the line spacing in your dissertation. If you don't, Word 2003 will insert extra white space before a line that includes a superscript and after a line that includes a subscript. See section 1.3.1.1.

5.2   Microsoft Equation Editor

For more complex equations and formulas, such as those using integral signs and radical symbols, you can use Microsoft Equation Editor, an equation editing program that is included in Word 2003 and some other Microsoft products such as PowerPoint.

To create an equation or formula with Microsoft Equation Editor, place your cursor at the point in the text where you want the equation or formula to appear. Click on **Insert** and **Object** and the **Create New** tab. From the **Object type** list, click once on **Microsoft Equation 3.0** to highlight it. Click **OK** (see Figure 5-3). Microsoft Equation Editor then will start.

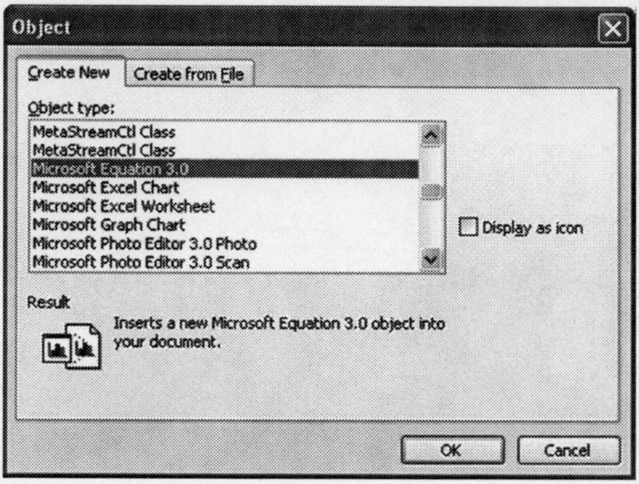

Figure 5-3

(If you do not see **Microsoft Equation 3.0** in the **Object type** list, then Equation Editor has not been installed on your computer. To install Equation Editor, quit Microsoft Word. Click once on the **Start** button at the bottom left corner of your screen. Then click once on **Control Panel** and twice on **Add or Remove Programs.** Under **Currently installed programs,** click once on either **Microsoft Office** or **Microsoft Office Word 2003** [depending on how you installed Word on your computer] and then on the **Change** button. Click once on the radio button next to **Add or Remove Features** and then on the **Next** button to bring up the **Advanced Customization** dialog box. Click on the plus sign to the left of **Office Tools** and then click on the icon to the left of **Equation Editor.** Select **Run from My Computer** and then click **Update.** Microsoft Equation Editor will be installed. You can restart Word and repeat the steps in the preceding paragraph.)

When you start Microsoft Equation Editor, it will deposit a box in your text at the point where your cursor was; the box is blank to start but is where you will place your equation or formula. A toolbar for Microsoft Equation Editor will appear; if the toolbar is blocking your view of text, it can be moved by grabbing the blue bar at the top of the toolbar with your mouse and dragging the toolbar to another part of your display. Menu options at the top of your screen also will change temporarily from the standard Word 2003 options to menu options for Microsoft Equation Editor.

(If you click outside the equation box, you will return to Word 2003, and the equation toolbar and menu options will disappear. To bring them back, simply double-click inside the equation box.)

5.2.1   Setting styles for your equations

Although Microsoft Equation Editor has default settings for the styles it uses to render equations and formulas, these styles are easily adjusted to meet your needs. Check your university's dissertation style manual and any disciplinary-specific style manuals that you are using for instructions on these format issues.

To set the font and font style of your equations, click on **Style** and **Define,** while Microsoft Equation Editor is running, to bring up the **Styles** dialog box (Figure 5-4). Here you can choose the font for eight different categories of text in your equations: text, functions, variables, uppercase Greek letters, lowercase Greek letters, symbols, matrices, and numbers. For each, you can choose a font using a drop-down menu, and you can use check boxes to indicate whether the font should be bold and/or italic. Click **OK** when you are done making your choices.

Styles					? X
Style	Font		Character Format		
			Bold	Italic	
Text	Times New Roman	▼	☐	☐	OK
Function	Times New Roman	▼	☐	☐	Cancel
Variable	Times New Roman	▼	☐	☑	
L.C. Greek	Symbol	▼	☐	☑	
U.C. Greek	Symbol	▼	☐	☐	
Symbol	Symbol	▼	☐	☐	
Matrix-Vector	Times New Roman	▼	☑	☐	
Number	Times New Roman	▼	☐	☐	

Figure 5-4

To set the font sizes of text in your equations, click on **Size** and **Define** to bring up the **Sizes** dialog box (Figure 5-5). This box allows you to set the size, in points, for regular text, superscripts and subscripts, super-superscripts and sub-subscripts, symbols, and subsymbols. (Keep in mind your university's requirements about minimum point sizes when setting these parameters. Some universities, for example, prohibit any text smaller than 10 points; if that is the case at your institution, you should use at least that value here.) Click **OK** when you are done.

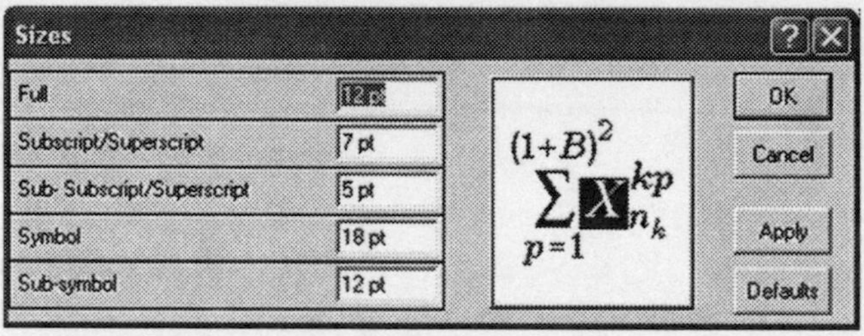

Figure 5-5

5.2.2 *Creating an equation*

To create an equation, click anywhere inside the equation box. (If you've closed Microsoft Equation Editor by clicking anywhere in the document outside the equation box, you can restart Microsoft Equation Editor by clicking twice anywhere inside the equation box.) You can add text to the box by typing it directly from the keyboard or by clicking on any of the buttons in the top row of the **Equation** toolbar (Figure 5-6). By clicking on any of the buttons in the bottom row of the **Equation** toolbar, you can add a variety of mathematical functions, such as integration and radicals. As you add elements to the equation box, Microsoft Equation Editor automatically adjusts the spacing between elements to provide a pleasing presentation; therefore, for example, you need not enter spaces between elements of an equation.

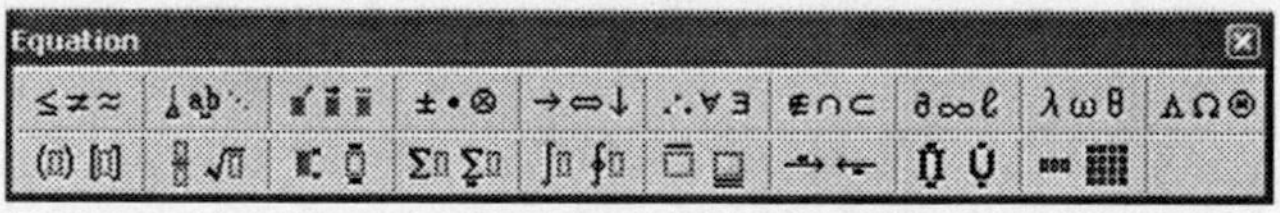

Figure 5-6

5.2.2.1 Symbol buttons

The ten buttons on the top of the **Equation** toolbar provide ways to add symbols to the equation box. To use any of the buttons, click once on top of the button. Then an extension to the button will open, listing all the possible symbols in that category. Single-click on the symbol that you want, and it will be added to the equation box. From left to right, the symbols available on the toolbar (Figure 5-6) are:

- Relational symbols, such as inequality and proportionality
- Spaces and ellipses, used for aligning equations
- Embellishments, or symbols such as primes and hats
- Operator symbols, such as arithmetic and algebraic operations
- Arrow symbols
- Logical symbols
- Set theory symbols
- Miscellaneous symbols
- Lowercase Greek letters
- Uppercase Greek letters

5.2.2.2   Templates

The nine buttons in the bottom row of the **Equation** toolbar provide differing ways of inserting mathematical functions and relationships into your equation box. (Microsoft Equation Editor calls these "templates," but they are not the same as Word 2003 templates, which control the look and feel of your word-processing documents. These templates provide a skeleton for writing mathematical relationships.)

As with the symbol boxes, click once on the desired box, and an extension of the box will appear with a variety of specific selections. Single-click on the selection that you want, and it will be added to the equation box. Unlike the addition of symbols, however, some templates include one or more "slots," or spots in which additional information such as numbers or variable names must be entered (such as the limits of integration, to go with an integration symbol). Each slot is denoted by a box marked with a dashed line; place your cursor into the slot and type or enter the necessary material.

The templates available on the bottom row of the toolbar (Figure 5-6), from left to right, are:

- Fence templates, or parentheses, brackets, and braces. You can put these symbols around existing material in an equation box by highlighting the text that you want surrounded and then adding the appropriate fence template. The template will be placed around the selected text and will be sized appropriately.
- Fraction and radical templates
- Subscripts and superscripts
- Sums
- Integrals
- Overbars and underbars
- Arrows
- Products and set theory relationships
- Matrices

5.2.3   Revising an equation

Material can be deleted from an equation by highlighting it and pressing the **Delete** key. You can delete a symbol, material in a slot in a template, a template, or an entire equation, depending on what you select.

You can also reformat part or all of your equation by highlighting it and then clicking on **Style** or **Size**. From **Style** you can select the correct style (see section 5.2.1) that you wish to be applied to the selection. From **Size** you can select the type of sizing that you want from the selection.

5.2.4   Saving the equation

When you are done creating the equation or formula, simply click anywhere outside the equation box. You will be returned to Word 2003, and the equation will be saved in the file when you next save the file.

5.2.5   Positioning the equation

You may want to move the equation from one location to another in your document. One easy way to do that is to select the object by clicking on it once. Then remove it from its current location by clicking on **Edit** and **Cut.** Next, move your cursor to the desired new location for the equation. Click on **Edit** and **Paste** to insert the equation.

5.2.6 *Adding a caption*

You may want to add a caption or title for your equations. Click once on the equation box for which you would like to add a caption by clicking on it once. Then click on **Insert** and then **Reference** and then **Caption**. The **Caption** dialog box will come up (Figure 5-7). From the **Label** drop-down menu, make sure that **Equation** is selected; if it is, the **Caption** box will have the word "Equation" followed by a number. From the **Position** drop-down menu, pick the location that your dissertation style manual prescribes for figure captions, whether above or below the item.

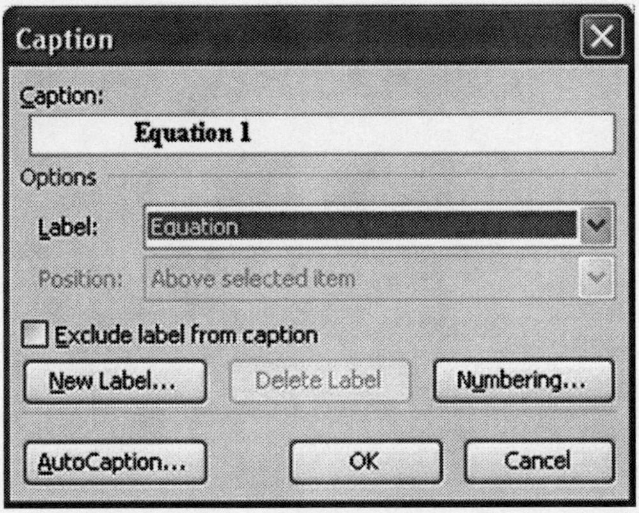

Figure 5-7

Then in the **Caption** box, type the remainder of your caption. (You may want to add a period or other punctuation after the figure number.) Then click **OK**, and the caption will be added to your text.

You cannot add special formatting to the caption (such as italics or boldface) in the **Caption** box. To change the formatting of a portion of your caption text, wait until you have clicked **OK** and the caption has been deposited in your dissertation text. Then you can reformat some or all of the caption as you wish and add special characters as well (see section 2.7).

Chapter 6

Back matter

The dissertation chapters are followed by the dissertation's back matter: appendices, bibliography, and the like. Creating these are, in most respects, quite similar to preparing the chapters of the dissertation.

6.1 Appendices

Appendices are optional, but most universities require that if appendices are used, they appear immediately after the body of the dissertation. If there is only one appendix, most universities dictate that it be titled "Appendix"; if there is more than one, they are generally either numbered (Appendix 1, Appendix 2, etc.) or lettered (Appendix A, Appendix B, etc.).

Each appendix should be its own Word 2003 file. To create an appendix file, click on **File** and then **New**. The **New Document** pane will open. In the **Templates** section, click once on **On my computer.** If you followed the instructions on saving your template in section 1.8, the **General** tab should include an icon labeled **My Dissertation**. Double-click on this icon, and Word 2003 will create a new document based on the template named **My Dissertation.**

6.1.1 Cover sheet

Some universities require or permit the use of a cover sheet—an otherwise blank page on which the title of the appendix appears.

To create a cover sheet, type the name of your appendix, whether simply "Appendix" or "Appendix 1" or "Appendix A." Type it as the first line of the file. Then, before hitting the **Enter** key, either type the shortcut key for the Heading 1 style (see section 1.4.1.4) or select **Heading 1** from the style drop-down menu in the **Formatting** toolbar (Figure 2-2). The text will be reformatted correctly. Now you can hit **Enter.**

If your university requires that the text on the cover sheet be centered vertically (that is, from top to bottom), place the cursor on the cover sheet title. Then click on **File** and **Page Setup**. In the **Page Setup** dialog box, click on the **Layout** tab. From the **Vertical alignment** drop-down menu, select **Center**, and from the **Apply to** drop-down menu, select **Whole document**. Click on **OK**. The title will look as if it's not in the center of your page, but when you print the page, the title will be in the center. Then turn off centering for the rest of your appendix by moving the cursor to the end of the file and again clicking on **File** and **Page Setup**. On the **Page Setup** dialog box, click on the **Layout** tab. From the **Vertical alignment** drop-down menu, select **Top**, and from the **Apply to** drop-down menu, select **This point forward**. Click on **OK**. This will insert a section break in the file, and only the text that appears before the section break will be centered vertically. There is no need to add a page break, because the section break will also start a new page.

However, if you did not center the cover sheet vertically, you must manually add a page break: Click **Insert** and then **Break** and then make sure that the **Page break** radio button is clicked. Click **OK**.

6.1.2   Appendix body

Now add the body of your appendix. If you did not add a cover sheet, type the name for your appendix, whether simply "Appendix" or "Appendix 1" or "Appendix A." Type it as the first line of the file. Then, before hitting **Enter**, either type the shortcut key for the Heading 1 style (see section 1.4.1.4) or select **Heading 1** from the style drop-down menu in the **Formatting** toolbar (Figure 2-2). The text will be reformatted correctly. Now you can hit **Enter.**

If your appendix consists of text, follow the same instructions that you followed for entering the body text of your dissertation (Chapter 2).

If the appendix contains a graphic image, follow the instructions in Chapter 4, and if the appendix contains tabular material, consult Chapter 3.

If your style rules require the first page of the appendix to have its page number in a different spot than other pages in the appendix, follow the instructions in section 1.2.2.

6.1.3   Saving the appendix file

When you are done creating the appendix, save it by clicking on **File** and then **Save As**. Using the **Save As** dialog box, navigate to the subdirectory where your other dissertation files are stored. In the **File name** field, enter a self-explanatory file name such as "Appendix" or "Appendix 1." Be sure that **Save as type** is set to **Word document (*.doc)**. Click on **OK** to save the document.

6.1.4   Revising an appendix file

To revise the appendix, simply open it: Click on **File** and then **Open**. Navigate to the subdirectory where your dissertation files are stored. Find the name of the appendix file in the list of files and double-click on it to open the file.

6.2   Notes

If you are using endnotes and have elected to gather them together at the end of your dissertation, rather than printing them at the end of each chapter, you must create a file for those endnotes.

To create a notes section for your dissertation, click on **File** and then **New**. The **New Document** pane will open. In the **Templates** section, click once on **On my computer.** If you followed the instructions on saving your template in section 1.8, the **General** tab should include an icon labeled **My Dissertation**. Double-click on this icon, and Word 2003 will create a new document based on the template named **My Dissertation**.

6.2.1   Cover sheet

If you wish to create a cover sheet for your endnotes, follow the directions for creating a cover sheet for your appendices (section 6.1.1) but of course use the correct name for your notes according to your style requirements—most likely, simply "Notes."

6.2.2 Notes body

Unlike other back matter files, there is no need to add any other information; Word 2003 will insert the notes automatically when the entire dissertation is assembled.

If your style rules require the first page of the notes section to have its page number in a different spot than other pages in the notes section, follow the instructions in section 1.2.2.

6.2.3 Saving the notes file

When you are done creating the notes file, save it by clicking on **File** and then **Save As**. Using the **Save As** dialog box, navigate to the subdirectory where your other dissertation files are stored. In the **File name** field, enter a self-explanatory file name such as "Notes." Be sure that **Save as type** is set to **Word document (*.doc)**. Click on **OK** to save the document.

6.2.4 Revising the notes file

To revise the notes file, click on **File** and then **Open**. Navigate to the subdirectory where your dissertation files are stored. Find the name of the notes file in the list of files and double-click on it to open the file.

6.3 Bibliography

Most universities require a dissertation to include a list of materials that were cited by the dissertation. This list goes by many names—some include "Bibliography," "List of References," and "Literature Cited." Check your institution's dissertation style manual to determine the preferred name for this list.

To create a bibliography section for your dissertation, click on **File** and then **New**. If you followed the instructions on saving your template in section 1.8, the **General** tab should include an icon labeled **My Dissertation**. Double-click on this icon, and Word 2003 will create a new document based on the template named **My Dissertation**.

6.3.1   Cover sheet

Some universities require or permit the use of a cover sheet—an otherwise blank page on which the title of the bibliography appears. Follow the directions for creating a cover sheet for your appendices (section 6.1.1) but of course instead use the correct name for your bibliography—"Bibliography" or "List of References," etc.—according to your style requirements.

6.3.2   Bibliography body

Now add the body of your bibliography. If you did not add a cover sheet, type the name for your bibliography, such as "Bibliography" or "List of References," according to your style requirements. Type it as the first line of the file. Then, before hitting the **Return** key, either type the shortcut key for the Heading 1 style (see section 1.4.1.4), or select **Heading 1** from the style drop-down menu in the **Formatting** toolbar. The text will be reformatted according to your dictates for the selected style. Now you can hit **Enter.**

Next, add the entries for your bibliography. By far, the easiest way to do this is with a third-party bibliographic program, such as EndNote or ProCite. These programs allow you to compile a database of references, insert them into your dissertation, and create a bibliography at the desired point in your dissertation. Although you may have to spend $100 to $200 for one of these programs (perhaps less through your campus bookstore), it will be well worth the time that you will save.

However, if you wish to create your bibliography manually, keep in mind that each entry should be a separate paragraph. Before hitting **Enter**, either type the shortcut key for the bibliography style that you created earlier (see section 1.5.8), or select **Bibliography** from the style drop-down menu in the **Formatting** toolbar. (If **Bibliography** isn't listed in the drop-down menu, click on **Format** and then on **Styles and Formatting.** In the **Styles and Formatting** pane, be sure that the **Show** drop-down menu is set to **Show to Custom...** to open the **Format Settings** dialog box. Under **Styles to be visible**, click in the box in front of **Bibliography**, so that a check mark appears in the box. Set the **Category** drop-down menu to **All styles**, and click on **OK** to close the **Format Settings** dialog box. Now you can choose it from the drop-down menu in the **Formatting** toolbar.) The text will be reformatted automatically. Now you can hit **Enter**. (Alternatively, you can enter multiple entries without setting their style. Then select all the entries and format them using the **Bibliography** shortcut key or drop-down menu entry.) A third-party bibliographic program will automatically alphabetize the bibliography, but you can manually alphabetize the entries by selecting all of the entries, then clicking on **Table** and then on **Sort.** In the **Sort Text** dialog box (Figure 6-1), be sure that **Paragraphs** is selected from the **Sort by** drop-down menu, that the **Type** is set to **Text**, and that the **Ascending** radio button is clicked. Click **OK** to sort the bibliography.

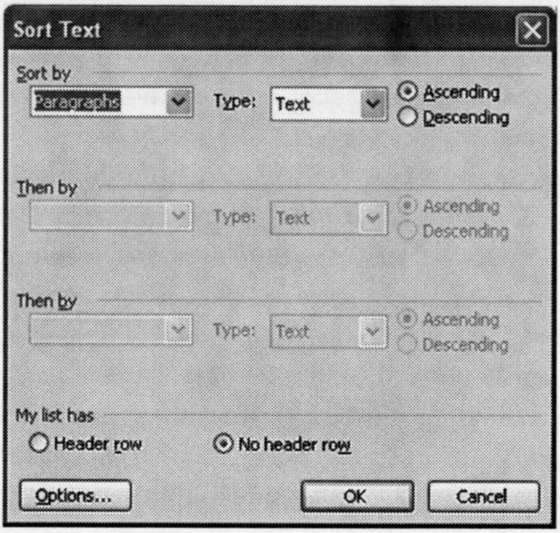

Figure 6-1

If your style rules require the first page of the bibliography to have its page number in a different spot than other pages in the bibliography, follow the instructions in section 1.2.2.

6.3.3   *Saving the bibliography file*

When you are done creating the bibliography, save it by clicking on **File** and then **Save As**. Using the **Save As** dialog box, navigate to the subdirectory where your other dissertation files are stored. In the **File**

name field, enter a self-explanatory file name such as "Bibliography." Be sure that **Save as type** is set to **Word document (*.doc)**. Click **OK** to save the document.

6.3.4 *Revising the bibliography*

To revise the bibliography, click on **File** and then **Open**. Navigate to the subdirectory where your dissertation files are stored. Find the name of the bibliography file in the list of files and double-click on it to open the file.

6.4   Vita

Some universities require that the last page of the dissertation be the author's vita, or academic résumé. Others request a biographical sketch. There often is a one-page limit on the vita or biographical sketch.

As with other parts of the back matter, the vita should be its own Word 2003 file. To create its file, click on **File** and then **New**. The **New Document** pane will open. In the **Templates** section, click once on **On my computer.** If you followed the instructions on saving your template in section 1.8, the **General** tab should include an icon labeled **My Dissertation**. Double-click on this icon, and Word 2003 will create a new document based on the template named **My Dissertation**.

If you are using cover sheets, follow the directions in section 6.1.1 for creating the cover sheet for the vita. If you did not add a cover sheet, type the title for your biographical information, whether "Biographical Sketch" or "Vita" or whatever is permitted by your graduate school. Type it as the first line of the file. Then, before hitting **Enter**, either type the shortcut key for the **Heading 1** style (see section 1.4.1.4) or select **Heading 1** from the style drop-down menu in the **Formatting** toolbar.

If your university requires that the vita not be listed in the table of contents, use the **Preliminary page** style instead of **Heading 1**. Click on **Format** and then on **Styles and Formatting.** In the **Styles and Formatting** pane, be sure that the **Show** drop-down menu is set to **All Styles**. Under **Pick formatting to** apply, look for an entry for **Preliminary page.** (If there is no listing for **Preliminary page,** set **Show** to **Custom...** to open the **Format Settings** dialog box. Set **Category** to **All styles.** Under **Styles to be visible**, click in the box in front of **Preliminary page**, so that a check mark appears in the box. Click on **OK** to close the **Format Settings** dialog box.) Now click once on **Preliminary page,** and the text will be reformatted.

Now press **Enter** and add the body of your biographical information. Select and reformat sections to conform to your university's dictates regarding presentation.

If your style rules require the vita to have its page number in a different spot than pages in the body of the dissertation, follow the instructions in section 1.2.2.

CHAPTER 7

Preliminary pages

The preliminary pages, sometimes also called the front matter, contain all the material that appears before the body of a dissertation: the title page, dedication, table of contents, and the like. Formatting rules for the preliminary pages often are different than formatting rules for the rest of the dissertation—for example, regarding page numbering—so be sure to check your university's formatting rules carefully.

To create a file to contain your preliminary pages, click on **File** and then **New.** The **New Document** pane will open. In the **Templates** section, click once on **On my computer.** If you followed the instructions on saving your template in section 1.8, the **General** tab should include an icon labeled **My Dissertation**. Double-click on this icon, and Word 2003 will create a new document based on the template named **My Dissertation.**

7.1 Pages without numbers

At many universities, the first few pages in the preliminary pages—for example, the title page, abstract page, and copyright page (if one is used)—do not have page numbers printed on them, but are counted when determining the page numbers of the preliminary pages that follow them that do have page numbers printed on them.

To handle this situation, we will break the preliminary pages into two sections: one without page numbers, and one with page numbers.

First, enter the material that should appear on preliminary pages without page numbers. Just as with your chapters, the text for your preliminary pages can be entered directly or copied from other files (sections 2.1 and 2.2).

Fonts and font sizes for the text can be altered by selecting the text in question and then clicking on **Format** and **Font** and making the desired changes. Line spacing (for example, for triple spacing between lines of the title, or to force a certain amount of white space before a specific line, if necessary) can be modified by selecting the text and clicking on **Format** and **Paragraph** and setting the **Line spacing** or **Before** fields to the desired value. Click **OK**.

To center text horizontally on a line, select it and either click on the **Center** button on the **Formatting** toolbar or click on **Format** and **Paragraph** and the **Indents and Spacing** tab. Set the **Alignment** drop-down menu to **Centered** and click **OK**.

When you wish to start a new page (say, between the title page and the dedication, if that is the order they are to appear in your document), click **Insert** and **Break** and **Page break** and then **OK**.

7.1.1   Copyright page

Many dissertations include a copyright page, which usually is unnumbered. To enter the copyright symbol ©, either type **(c)**, and AutoCorrect will change the characters to **©,** or hold down the **ALT** key and use the numeric keyboard on the side of the keyboard, with **Num Lock** turned on (not the number keys at the top of the keyboard) to type **0169**. Windows will translate those keystrokes into the symbol ©.

To center the copyright statement vertically on the page, if your university requires it, you must place the copyright page in its own section in the document. If you've placed an ordinary page break before or after the copyright statement, delete them. Then place the cursor immediately before the copyright statement. Click on **File** and **Page Setup** and click on the **Layout** tab. From the **Section start** drop-down menu, pick **New page**. From the **Vertical alignment** drop-down menu, pick **Center**. From the **Apply to** drop-down menu, pick **This point forward**. Click **OK**.

This creates a new page, with the copyright statement centered on it. But now you must un-center the portion of the preliminary pages that follows the copyright page. Place your cursor immediately after the copyright statement. Click on **File** and **Page Setup** and click on the **Layout** tab. From the **Section start** drop-down menu, pick **New page**. From the **Vertical alignment** drop-down menu, pick **Top**. From the **Apply to** drop-down menu, pick **This point forward**. Click **OK**.

After you have finished adding the material that should appear on unnumbered pages, create a new section for the numbered preliminary pages: Click **Insert** and **Break**, and under **Section break types,** click on **Next page** and **OK**. This creates a new section and automatically positions your cursor at the start of the new, second section.

Now click on **View** and then on **Header and Footer**. Word 2003 will display the header for your new section, along with the **Header and Footer** toolbar. If your page numbers are on the upper right or upper center of each page, leave your cursor in the header. If your page numbers are on the bottom right or bottom center of each page, scroll down to the footer and click once in it. On the **Header and Footer** toolbar, click once on the **Link to Previous** button (Figure 3-17) to tell Word 2003 that the header or footer (depending on where your page numbers are placed) in the second section should not be the same as the header or footer in the first section. Then click on the **Show Previous** button (Figure 3-18) to move to the header or footer of the first section (the one that you want to not have page numbers). Use your cursor to highlight the page number in the header or footer of the first section. Click on the **Delete** key to eliminate the page number. Click on the **Close** button in the **Header and Footer** toolbar.

As a general rule, the preliminary pages that do have numbers use lowercase Roman numerals (i, ii, iii, etc.) rather than Arabic numerals (1, 2, 3, etc.). But your dissertation template is configured for Arabic numbers. To change from Arabic to Roman in the numbered preliminary pages, take these steps: Place your cursor anywhere in the second section of your preliminary pages. Click on **Insert** and then **Page Numbers**. In the **Page Numbers** dialog box, click on the **Format** button. In the **Page Number Format** dialog box, choose **i, ii, iii, ...** from the **Number format** drop-down menu. In the **Page numbering** section, click on the **Start at** radio button and make sure that the value in the box following it is set to **i**. Click **OK** twice to close all dialog boxes.

7.1.2   Abstract

In many universities, the unnumbered pages section of the preliminary pages includes an abstract of the dissertation. Often there is a limit on the length of the abstract. You can determine the number of words in the abstract by highlighting the abstract. Then click **Tools** and **Word Count**. Word 2003 will provide a number of statistics about the highlighted passage, including the number of words (Figure 7-1).

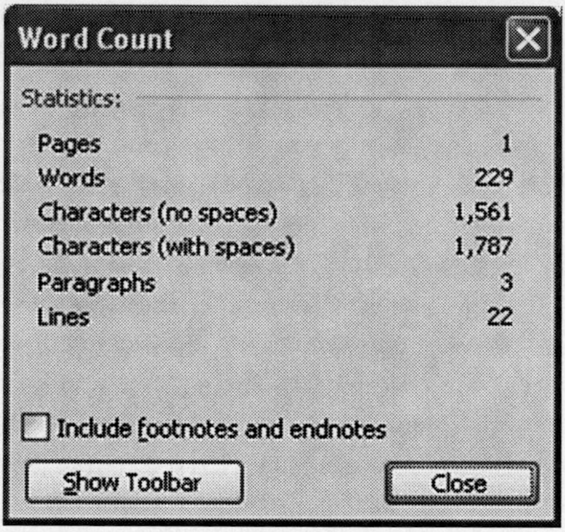

Word Count

Statistics:	
Pages	1
Words	229
Characters (no spaces)	1,561
Characters (with spaces)	1,787
Paragraphs	3
Lines	22

☐ Include footnotes and endnotes

[Show Toolbar]   [Close]

Figure 7-1

7.2   Pages with numbers

The numbered preliminary pages generally include the dedication, acknowledgments, preface, table of contents, list of tables, list of figures, list of equations, and list of symbols. Your dissertation may not have all these elements. Your university may have specific rules regarding the order in which they must appear in your dissertation, so check your university's formatting rules.

First, enter the material that should appear on preliminary pages without page numbers. Just as with your chapters, the text for your preliminary pages can be entered directly or copied from other files (sections 2.1 and 2.2).

To start a new page, click **Insert** and **Break** and **Page break** and then **OK**.

Then type the title for the page, such as "Dedication." Before hitting **Enter,** either type the shortcut key for the Heading 1 style (see section 1.4.1.4), or select **Heading 1** from the style drop-down menu in the **Formatting** toolbar.

Add the remainder of the text for the page. If you wish it to be formatted like your dissertation's body text, highlight the text and select **Normal** from the style drop-down menu in the **Formatting** toolbar. Fonts and font sizes for the text can be altered by selecting the text in question and then clicking on **Format** and **Font** and making the desired changes. Line spacing (for example, for triple spacing between lines of the title or to force a certain amount of white space before a specific line, if necessary) can be modified by selecting the text and clicking on **Format** and **Paragraph** and setting the **Line spacing** or **Before** fields to the desired value. Click **OK**.

To center text horizontally on a line, select it and either click on the center button on the **Formatting** toolbar or click on **Format** and **Paragraph** and the **Indents and Spacing** tab. Set the **Alignment** drop-down menu to **Center** and click **OK**.

7.3   Creating a table of contents

If you followed the directions in Chapter 1 about the styles for chapter titles, major headings, and minor headings, and if you used those headings in your manuscript (rather than, for example, simply typing an all-uppercase line of text as a heading without applying the heading style to it), then creating your table of contents will be relatively easy.

7.3.1   First steps

First, create a new page for the table of contents: Click **Insert**, then **Break**, then **Page break**, and finally **OK**.

Then type the title for the table of contents. Most universities direct you to use, not surprisingly, "Table of Contents." Before hitting **Enter**, either type the shortcut key for the Heading 1 style (see section 1.4.1.4) or select **Heading 1** from the style drop-down menu in the **Formatting**. The text will be reformatted according to your dictates for the selected style. Now you can hit **Enter** and leave your cursor on the new line.

Click **Insert** and then **Reference** and then **Index and Tables**, which will bring up the **Index and Tables** dialog box. Click on the **Table of Contents** tab (Figure 7-2).

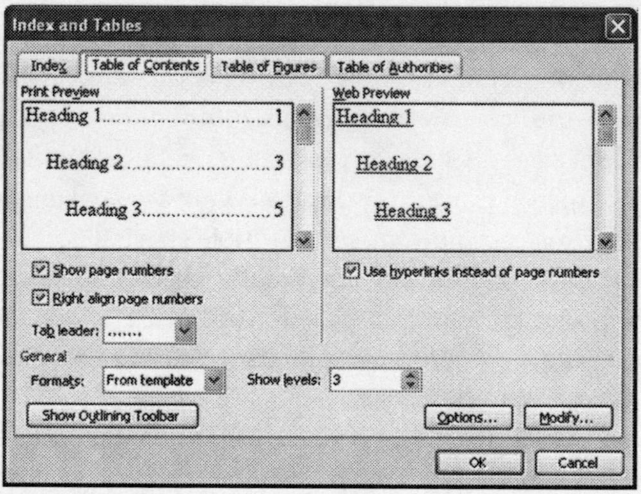

Figure 7-2

Word 2003's default configuration for generating a table of contents contains all headings that have been formatted with Heading 1, Heading 2, or Heading 3 style. The default configuration also includes page numbers along the right margin and a line of dots (called a "dot leader" or a "tab leader") between each entry in the table of contents and its page number. The default configuration formats the text in the default font that you specified in your template (section 1.3).

You can alter these options. But first consult your dissertation style manual regarding formatting requirements for the table of contents.

7.3.2 Table levels

You can select how many levels of headings are included in your table of contents. By default, Word 2003 includes three levels of headings, which in this context would mean chapter titles, major divisions of chapters, and the first level of minor divisions. You can instruct Word 2003 to include more, or fewer, levels of headings by selecting or typing the desired number in the **Show levels** box.

7.3.3   Table format

Word 2003 has a number of built-in styles for tables of contents. You can examine them by selecting choices from the **Formats** drop-down menu. However, each of these uses a variety of type styles and fonts, which may not comport well with the requirements of your dissertation style manual. The best option probably is to select **From template**, which will ensure that the table uses the default and font size specified in your template (which you selected in section 1.3 to agree with your dissertation requirements). The **Preview** box shows an example of how your table of contents will look (although it does not show actual headings from your dissertation).

However, you may still need to make some revisions to the table of contents formatting in relation to indentation and line spacing.

On the **Table of Contents** tab, click on the **Modify** button to bring up the **Style** dialog box (Figure 7-3). In its left-hand pane, it lists styles for various levels of the table of contents.

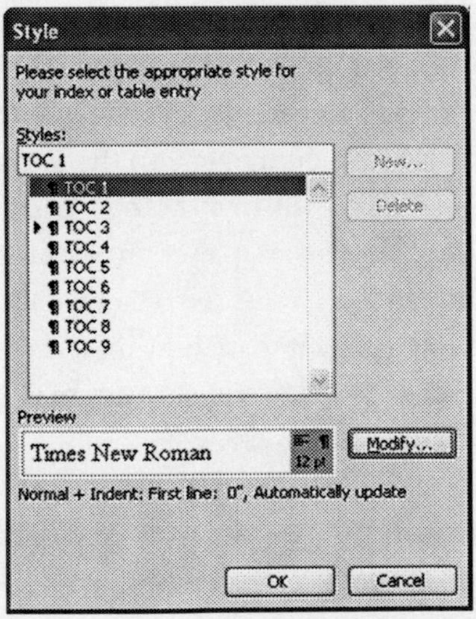

Figure 7-3

1. To modify the style for top-level headings in the table of contents, click once on the **TOC 1** listing to highlight it and then click on the **Modify** button to bring up the **Modify Style** dialog box (Figure 7-4).

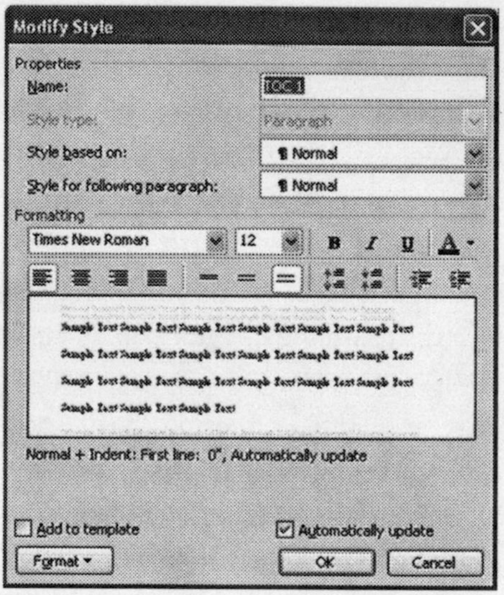

Figure 7-4

2. If you want your the first-level table of contents entries to have different font characteristics than the default (bold, italic, or a different font or font size), click on the **Format** button, then on **Font,** set the appropriate values on the **Font** tab, and click **OK.**

3. If you want first-level entries in the table to have different line spacing than the default, click on the **Format** button, then on **Paragraph.** Set the **Line spacing** drop-down menu to the amount of spacing that you want between lines of a single table of contents entry, or use the **Exactly** setting if you have been doing so elsewhere in your dissertation (section 1.3.1.1). Set the **Before** option to the amount of spacing that you want before each entry. Click **OK** when done.

4. To indent your table of contents entries, click on the **Paragraph** button. Set **Left** to the amount of indentation that you desire. Click **OK** when done.

5. When you are done configuring **TOC 1**, be sure the **Add to template** box is checked in the **Modify Style** dialog box, and click **OK** to return to the **Style** dialog box.

Repeat steps 1 through 5 for other levels of the tables of contents that you plan to use: **TOC 2**, **TOC3**, and so forth. (You need not configure levels that you do not expect to use; for example, if you will only use three levels of entries, you need not modify TOC 4.) Each level can be formatted differently. For example, you may not want to indent your first-level entries at all, but you may want to indent second-level entries by a certain amount and third-level entries by even more.

When you are done configuring all styles for the table of contents, click **Apply** in the **Style** dialog box to return to the **Index and Tables** dialog box.

7.3.4 Page numbers

You can uncheck the **Show page numbers** box if you want the table of contents not to include page numbers. However, most universities require page numbers in the table of contents, so you should probably leave this box checked.

If you check the **Right align page numbers** box, the page number for each entry in the table of contents will appear along the right margin. If you uncheck this box, the page number will appear immediately to the right of the entry.

7.3.5 Tab leader

If your table of contents uses right-aligned page numbers, it will insert the tab leader between each entry in the table of contents and its page number. For example, if **Tab leader** is set to **......**, a line of periods will be inserted. You can select periods, dashes, underlines, or **(none)** if you want no tab leader. (If you are not using right-aligned page numbers, this option has no effect.)

7.3.6 Creating the table of contents

After you have selected the desired options for your table of contents, click **OK**. The table will be added to your document at the cursor's location. It will be black text on a gray background, which is Word 2003's way of signaling that the table is not standard text; rather, it is a "field" that can be updated as information changes elsewhere in the document.

If you insert the table of contents in a file that does not yet contain any headings, the list field will contain the words **"Error! No table of contents entries found."** This is not worrisome and will be corrected after you merge your front matter with the body of your dissertation.

7.3.7   *Editing the results*

Proofread the table of contents carefully. Check that all headings are included. If some are missing, double-check the heading in the text. Make sure that the correct heading style has been applied to the heading in question. You can edit the entries and even delete some, but be cautious in doing so, because many universities require that the table of contents entries be exactly the same as the corresponding headings in the text.

7.3.8   *Updating your table of contents*

Sometimes you may need to update your table of contents. For example, you may add some additional text that changes the page numbers of subsequent headings in the table of contents.

To update the table, click once anywhere in the table and then press the **F9** key. You will get a dialog box that asks whether you want to update only the page numbers or the entire table. If you update the entire table, you will lose any manual revisions to the table that you have made, as described in the previous section, so choose this option if you have not added any new headings to the dissertation. If you update only the page numbers, Word 2003 will retain the previous entries in the table of contents, including any manual changes, and will simply revise their page numbers. Click **OK** after making your choice.

You may also want to change the format of your table of contents. Perhaps you want wider indentations, or you want to change the fonts.

Position your cursor anywhere within the table of contents. Then click on **Insert** and then **Reference** and then **Index and Tables**, which will bring up the **Index and Tables** dialog box. Click on the **Table of Contents** tab. Follow the formatting steps in sections 7.3.2 through 7.3.5. When you've finished selecting your new formatting options, click on **OK** in the **Table of Contents** tab. Word 2003 will ask "**Do you want to replace the selected table of contents?**" Click **OK**, and the table of contents will be replaced with a newly formatted version. You will have to repeat any editing that you performed on the previous version (section 7.3.7).

7.4   Lists of tables, figures, and equations

You can also create lists of tables, figures, and equations. These typically are in the text immediately after the table of contents. At this point, we simply determine the formatting and location of these lists in the document; in the next chapter, you will instruct Word to actually generate the lists of page numbers.

To start a new page for a list, position your cursor immediately after the table of contents, click **Insert** and **Break** under **Section break types**, click the **Next page** radio button and click **OK**.

Then type the title for the list, such as "List of Tables." Before hitting **Enter**, either type the shortcut key for the Heading 1 style (see section 1.4.1.4) or select **Heading 1** from the style drop-down menu in the **Formatting** toolbar. The text will be reformatted according to your dictates for the selected style. Now you can hit **Enter** and leave your cursor on the new line.

7.4.1   First steps

Click **Insert** and then **Reference** and then **Index and Tables**, which will bring up the **Index and Tables** dialog box. Click on the **Table of Figures** tab (Figure 7-5). (And yes, "Table of Figures" is correct here, even if you are compiling a list of tables or equations rather than a list of figures.)

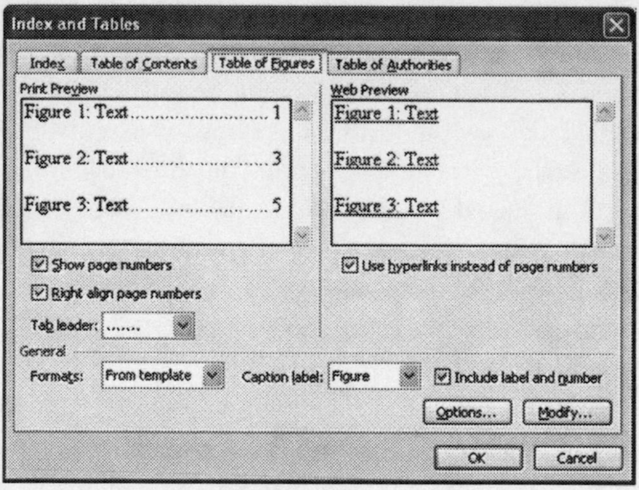

Figure 7-5

From the **Caption label** drop-down menu, select the type of list you are trying to create: **Equation** for a list of equations, Figure for a list of figures, **Map** for a list of maps, or **Table** for a list of tables.

If you uncheck the box **Include label and number**, each entry in the list will contain only the caption (or title), not the number, of the figure or table or equation that you gave it when you created it (sections 3.3 and 4.4). If the box is checked, the title will be prefaced with the appropriate figure category and number, for example "Table 1:" or "Figure 2:".

The other formatting options are identical to those available in creating a table of contents. For the sake of consistent formatting, you should make selections for **Show page numbers** and **Right align page numbers** and **Tab leader** and **Formats** that are identical to those you used in your table of contents. The **Preview** box shows how the text will look with the options that you have selected.

7.4.2   Modifying the formatting

However, you may still need to make some revisions to the table of contents formatting and deal with such matters as indentation and line spacing. On the **Table of Contents** tab, click on the **Modify** button to bring up the **Style** dialog box (Figure 7-6). Click the **Modify** button on this dialog box as well to get the **Modify Style** page (Figure 7-7).

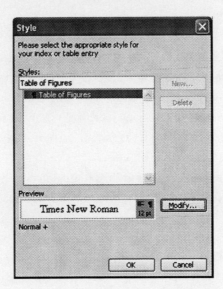

Figure 7-6

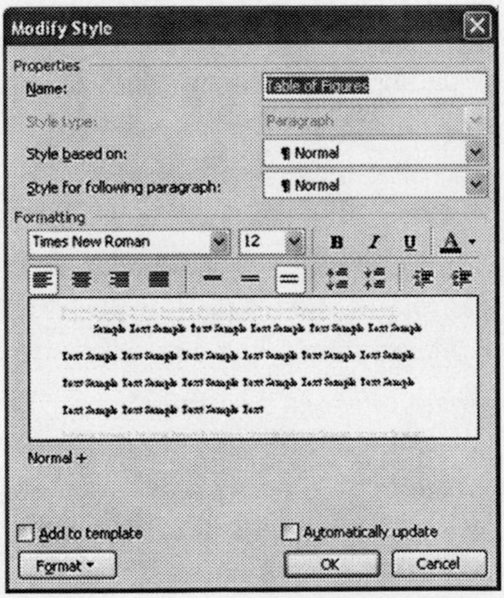

Figure 7-7

If you want your lists of equations, figures, and tables to have different font characteristics than the default (bold, italic, or a different font or font size), click on the **Format** button, then on **Font**, set the appropriate values on the **Font** tab, and click **OK**.

If you want to modify the line spacing in your lists of equations, figures, and tables, click on the **Format** button, then on **Paragraph**. Set the **Line spacing** drop-down menu to the amount of spacing that you want between lines of a single entry or use the **Exactly** setting if you have been doing so elsewhere in your dissertation (section 1.3.1.1). Set the **Before** option to the amount of spacing that you want before an entry. Click **OK** when done.

To indent the entries in your lists of equations, figures, and tables, click on the **Format** button, then on **Paragraph**. Set **Left** to the amount of indentation that you desire. Click **OK** when done.

When you are done configuring the list style, be sure the **Add to template** box is checked in the **Modify Style** dialog box, and click **OK** to return to the **Style** dialog box. Then click **OK** in the **Style** dialog box to return to the **Index and Tables** dialog box.

7.4.3 Inserting the list

When you have selected your formatting options, click **OK** in the **Index and Tables** dialog box, and the desired list will be added to your document. If you are changing the formatting of an existing list, Word will ask **"Do you want to replace the selected table of figures?"** Click **OK** again.

Like the table of contents, the list will be black text on a gray background, signifying that it is a field. And like the table of contents, entries in lists of figures, tables, and equations can be edited, such as shortening an entry or italicizing a phrase.

If you insert the list in a file that does not yet contain any entries for that list—for example, if you insert a list of tables in a document that does not have any tables—the list field will contain the phrase **"Error! No table of figures entries found."** This is not worrisome and can be corrected when you merge your front matter with the body of your dissertation.

If you wish to add another list—say, a list of tables in addition to a list of figures—simply repeat the process: Create a new page, add a title, and insert the appropriate list using the **Table of Figures** dialog box.

7.4.4   Custom lists

By default, Word 2003 is configured to be able to create lists for only equations, figures, and tables. But if you create new caption categories of your own (section 4.7), Word 2003 can create lists of items in those categories. For example, if you create a caption category called Maps, and enter one or more Map captions in your dissertation, Word 2003 can create a list of maps. Follow the steps described in this section, but when choosing a selection from the **Caption label** drop-down menu, select the caption type that you created, such as **Maps**.

7.4.5   Updating a list

As with tables of contents, you may need to update your lists of equations, figures, and tables if page numbers in your dissertation change. To update a list, click once anywhere in it, and then press the **F9** key. You will get a dialog box that asks whether you want to update only the page numbers or the entire table. If you update the entire list, you will lose any manual revisions to entries in the list that you have made. If you update only the page numbers, Word 2003 will retain the previous entries in the list, including any manual changes, and will simply revise their page numbers. Click **OK** after making your choice.

As with your table of contents, you may decide that you want to tinker with the format of your lists. Position your cursor anywhere within the list. Then click on **Insert** and then **Reference** and then **Index and Tables**, which will bring up the **Index and Tables** dialog box. Click on the **Table of Figures** tab. Follow the formatting steps in sections 7.4.1 and 7.4.2. When you've finished selecting your new formatting options, click on **OK** in the **Table of Figures** tab. Word 2003 will ask "**Do you want to replace the selected table of figures?**" Click **OK**, and all your lists of equations, figures, and tables will be replaced with newly formatted versions. You will have to repeat any editing that you performed on the previous versions.

7.5   Saving your preliminary pages

When you've completed creating your preliminary pages, you must save them. Go to the **File** menu and select **Save As**. In the dialog box, type a name for the file (here, and throughout the book, we will call it **Preliminary Pages**), and from the **Save as type** pull-down menu, select **Word Document (*.doc)**. Using the **Save In** box, navigate to the location where you are saving your dissertation files. Click on **OK**.

7.6   Revising your preliminary pages

To revise your preliminary pages file, click on **File** and then on **Open**. Using the **Look in** box, navigate to the folder that contains your dissertation files. Click on **Preliminary Pages** (assuming that's the name you gave it). After making any revisions, be sure to save the revised file, following the instructions in section 7.5.

Chapter 8

Putting it all together

Once you have completed the chapters, back matter, and preliminary pages for your dissertation, it's time to combine them so that you can create the dissertation's bibliography, get the page numbers correct, and take care of other tasks that you cannot efficiently do when the dissertation is broken into pieces.

There are two ways to merge the segments of your dissertation: You can create a single Word file into which all the parts of the dissertation have been merged, or you can create a "master document," a special type of Word 2003 file that allows you to simultaneously edit many files—such as the chapters of your dissertation—as if they were merged together.

Creating a single file has the advantage of generating a single word processing file that is easily moved from one computer to another and easily e-mailed to others. However, it does offer some disadvantages. For one thing, because you are putting all your eggs in one basket, you could risk losing your entire dissertation if the file becomes corrupted. Another consideration is that if your dissertation is a large file, Word 2003 may slow down.

The master document approach may make more sense if you plan to distribute drafts of individual chapters of your dissertation to your committee members. You could e-mail the member only the chapters that they need and then incorporate their suggestions in your subdocument files. However, some users feel that Word's master document system is prone to bugs, so if you go this route, be extra certain that you are frequently backing up your files.

8.1 Creating a single, merged file

1. To create a merged file for your dissertation, open the file that has your preliminary pages. Following the steps below, add the other individual dissertation files to this file. Place your cursor at the end of the first file of your dissertation (probably your preliminary pages).

2. Add a section break before the file that you're going to add by clicking on **Insert** and **Break** and **Next page** and then clicking **OK**.

3. Add the next individual dissertation file (probably Chapter1.doc) by clicking on **Insert** and then **File** (see Figure 8-1). Navigate to the drive and directory in which your dissertation files reside. Highlight the name of the file that you want to add. Click **Insert**.

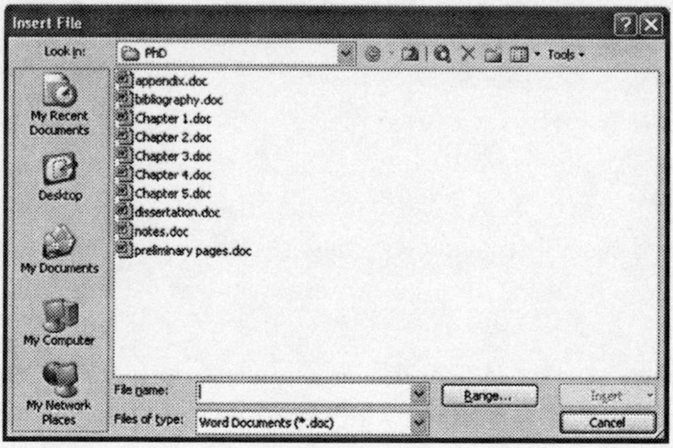

Figure 8-1

4. Stop for a moment after you have added the first file that will be numbered with Arabic page numbers (probably Chapter 1). You must reset the numbering to 1 in this section. To do this, be sure that your cursor is placed in the first page of Chapter 1. Then click **Insert** and **Page Numbers** and click on the **Format** button. Be sure that **Number Format** is set to **1, 2, 3...** (it should be set to this

already), and make sure that 1 is entered in the **Start at** field (Figure 8-2). Click **OK** twice.

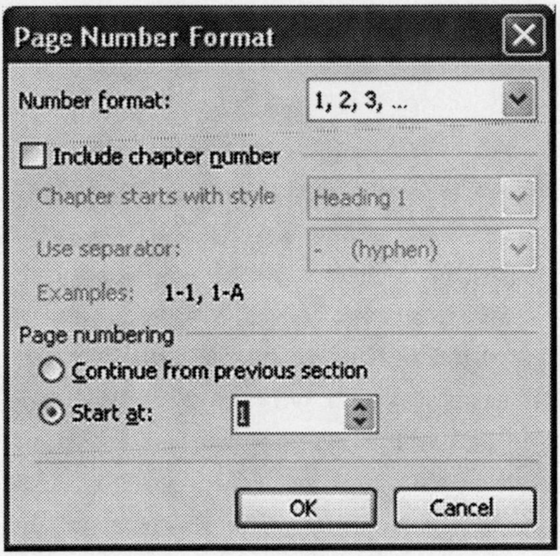

Figure 8-2

5. Move on to the other chapters, and finally add your back matter files (bibliography.doc, vita.doc, appendix1.doc, etc.).

If you are using a third-party bibliographic program (section 6.3), stop adding files once you have added the blank page for your bibliography. Use your bibliographic program to create the bibliography. Then resume the process with any material that should appear after the bibliography.

As section 2.4.3 indicated, gathering endnotes at the end of the dissertation is a problem in Word 2003 because, in most dissertations, there is additional material that must appear after the endnotes. The solution is to create two files: one that includes all files from the start of the dissertation through the endnotes and a second that includes only the files that contain information that should appear after the endnotes. When printing this second section, be sure to set its starting page to the page number following the endnotes. (To do this, click **Insert** and **Page Numbers** and the **Format** button. Set **Start at** to the appropriate page number. Click **OK** twice.)

When you are done merging files, save the merged dissertation file by clicking on **File** and **Save As**. Navigate to the drive and directory where you save your dissertation files. Type a name for the file, such as **Dissertation,** and be sure that **Save as type** is set to **Word document (*.doc)**. Click **OK.**

8.2 Creating a master document

In Word 2003, a "master document" is a special document that contains links to one or more other Word 2003 files, called "subdocuments." To create a master document for your dissertation, click on **File, New,** and then **On my computer**. If you followed the instructions on saving your template in section 1.8, the **General** tab should include an icon labeled **My Dissertation.** Double-click on this icon, and Word 2003 will create a new document based on the template named **My Dissertation.**

Now switch to **Outline View** by clicking on **View** and **Outline**. The **Outlining** toolbar will come up, which includes buttons for managing your master document and its subdocuments.

- For each dissertation file that you want to add as a subdocument, first click on the **Insert Subdocument** icon (Figure 8-3). Navigate to the file that you want to add and highlight it (Figure 8-4), and click on **Open**. If the file has a template that differs from your **My Dissertation** template, you will get a warning message about that fact.

Figure 8-3

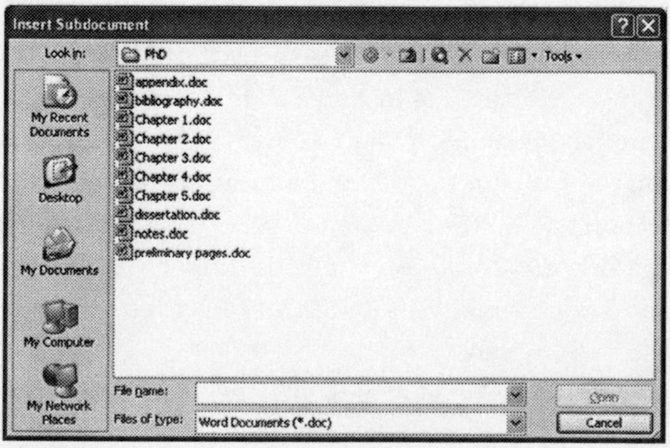
Insert Subdocument
Look in:
PhD
Tools
appendix.doc
bibliography.doc
Chapter 1.doc
Chapter 2.doc
Chapter 3.doc
Chapter 4.doc
Chapter 5.doc
dissertation.doc
notes.doc
preliminary pages.doc
My Recent Documents
Desktop
My Documents
My Computer
My Network Places
File name:
Files of type:
Word Documents (*.doc)
Open
Cancel

Figure 8-4

- If you are using a third-party bibliographic program (section 6.3), stop adding files after you have added the file for your bibliography. Use your bibliographic program to create the bibliography. Then resume adding any files that should appear after the bibliography.
- You can collapse the display of the text of the subdocuments into a single line, listing the file name of each subdocument file, by clicking on the **Collapse Subdocuments** icon (Figure 8-5). You can likewise expand the collapsed display by clicking on the **Expand Subdocuments** icon (Figure 8-6).

Figure 8-5

Figure 8-6

- If you wish to delete a subdocument from the master file, click on **Collapse Subdocuments**, click on the subdocument icon (Figure 8-7) next to the subdocument you want to delete, and then press the **Delete** key. (Note: The file remains on your hard disk, although the link to it from the master document has been removed.)

Figure 8-7

- To move a subdocument from one location to another, click on **Collapse Subdocuments**, click on the subdocument icon (Figure 8-7) next to the subdocument you want to delete, and drag it to the desired location.

  As section 2.4.3 indicated, gathering endnotes at the end of the dissertation is a problem in Word 2003 because, in most dissertations, there is additional material that must appear after the endnotes. The solution is to create two master documents: one including all files from the start of the dissertation through the endnotes and a second including only the files that contain information that should appear after the endnotes. When printing this second master document, be sure to set its starting page to the page number following the endnotes. (To do this, click **Insert** and **Page Numbers** and the **Format** button. Set **Start at** to the appropriate page number. Click **OK** twice.)

Once you have inserted all your subdocuments into the master document, you can switch to the more familiar **Normal** view by clicking on **View** and **Normal**. Your master document will appear as if it is a single document, without the subdocuments being identified as such. (If you wish to manage the subdocuments, such as adding more subdocuments, you must switch back to **Outline** view, as above.)

Because your document starts out with Roman numbering but must switch to Arabic numerals, you must manually make this switch. Click on **View** and **Normal**, and then on the first page of the first portion of your dissertation that is to include Arabic page numbers (probably Chapter 1). Then click **Insert** and **Page Numbers** and click on the **Format** button. Be sure that **Number Format** is set to **1, 2, 3...** (it should be set to this already), and make sure that **1** is entered in the **Start at** field (Figure 8-2). Click **OK** twice.

Be sure to save the master document and the subdocuments before quitting Word 2003: Click **Ctrl** and **S** simultaneously or click on **File** and **Save**. If this is the first time that you have saved the master document file, Word 2003 will bring up the **Save As** dialog box, and you should navigate to the drive and directory where your dissertation files are stored and enter a file name for the master document, such as **Dissertation**. Click **OK**. Word 2003 will save both the master document and its subdocuments.

8.3   A few last things to check

You're probably very eager to print out the dissertation, but before you do so, take a few minutes for some last things to check:

8.3.1   *Inserting and updating cross-references*

If you wanted to insert cross-references (section 2.8) from one chapter of your dissertation to another, now is the time to do so. With all the chapters merged together, either as a single document or through a master document, the **Insert cross-reference** command will show all the headings, tables, and figures to which you can add cross-reference fields.

If you entered cross-references earlier, you should update them, to account for material that you may have added to the dissertation after you inserted the cross-references. Word 2003 does not automatically update the cross-reference fields as you edit the document. For example, if you insert a cross-reference to Table 2 and then add some additional tables prior to Table 2 so that it becomes Table 5, the cross-reference to the table's number will not automatically be updated from 2 to 5. Instead, you must instruct Word 2003 to update the cross-reference fields. To update a single cross-reference in your document, click anywhere in the cross-reference's field (marked by the gray background) and press the **F9** key. To update all cross-references and other fields in your document, select the whole document by pressing the **Ctrl** and **A** keys simultaneously and then press the **F9** key.

You also may want to configure your printing function so that any printouts automatically include updated cross-references. To do this, click on **Tools**, then **Options**, and then the **Print** tab. In the **Printing options** section, make sure that the **Update fields** box is checked. Click on **OK** (see Figure 8-8).

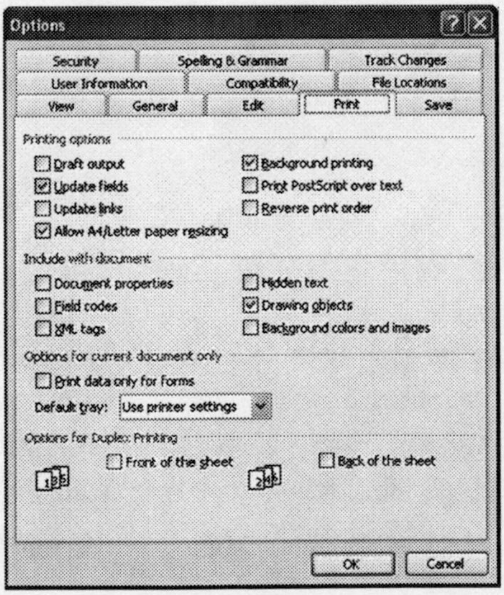

Figure 8-8

8.3.2   Check spelling

Spell-check your dissertation by pressing the **F7** key, which starts Word's grammar and spell checker. Word 2003 will check your entire document, looking for potentially misspelled words. For each possible error, Word 2003 will display a dialog box (Figure 8-9) listing the error, in red, with some of the surrounding text. If Word 2003 can offer one or more possible corrections, they are listed under **Suggestions**. If you wish to accept one of the suggestions, highlight it and click either **Change** (if you want to change only this instance of the error) or **Change All** (if you want to change the error anywhere it appears in your dissertation). If you want to make the change *and* add the correction to the AutoCorrect database (section 2.7), click on **AutoCorrect**.

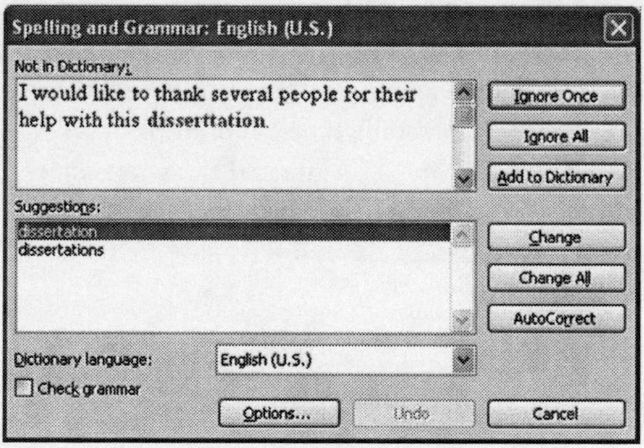

Figure 8-9

On the other hand, you might not want to make the change because the word is correctly spelled even though Word 2003 doesn't recognize it. If you do not wish to change the highlighted word, click **Ignore Once** (if you want to accept the word only in this location of the document) or **Ignore All** (if you want to accept the word throughout your dissertation). If you wish to accept the word *and* have it added to Word 2003's dictionary, click **Add to Dictionary**.

For a dissertation, the box **Check grammar** should probably be unchecked, because Word 2003's grammar checker does not seem to handle academic prose very well.

After Word's spelling checker has been through your document once and made changes to the document, it may refuse to check the document again, telling you instead that the spelling check is complete (Figure 8-10). To instruct Word 2003 to recheck the document, click on **Tools** and **Options** and then the **Spelling & Grammar** tab (Figure 8-11). Click on the **Recheck Document** button. You will be presented with a confirmation dialog. Click **Yes** and then **OK** and then perform the spell check again by clicking **F7**.

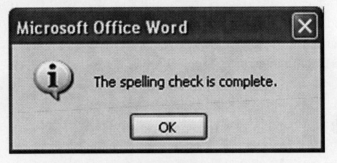

Figure 8-10

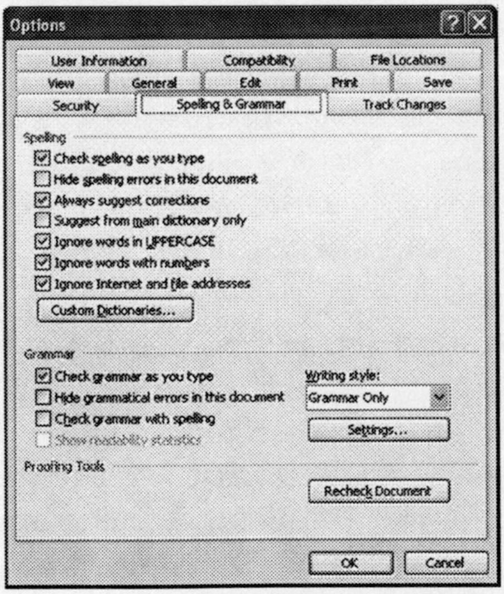

Figure 8-11

8.3.3   Positioning of tables

If you use tables in your dissertation, check the placement of each one. Make sure that a table that could be on one page isn't needlessly split across two pages. In such a case, you might want to move some text from before the table to after it, or you might want to insert a manual page break before the table so that it is on one page: To insert a manual page break, position your cursor where you want the page break to go. Then click on **Insert** and **Break** and **Page break** and **OK**.

8.3.4   Check widows and orphans

If your university discourages or forbids the appearance of widows and orphans in a dissertation, make sure that your document does not contain any. Switch to **Print Layout** view by clicking on **View** and **Print Layout**. This will display your document exactly as it will appear when printed, including headers, footers, and page breaks.

Scroll through the document, looking for widows and orphans. Word 2003 can prevent most widows and orphans if you have configured your style to do so (section 1.4.2.3). But Word 2003 is unable to automatically fix one particular kind of orphan: Many universities require that a heading at the bottom of a dissertation page be followed by at least two lines of text before the page break, but Word 2003 cannot identify this kind of error. If your university has such a two-line requirement, start at the beginning of your dissertation and slowly scroll through it, checking the bottom of each page for a violation of the rule. If you find one line of text after a heading, place your cursor at the beginning of the line on which the heading appears. Force a page break at that point by clicking **Insert** and **Break** and **Page break** and **OK**. This will leave a few blank lines at the bottom of the page, but most universities prefer blank lines to an orphan.

8.3.5   Update the table of contents

Make sure that your table of contents has correct page numbers by updating it. Click once anywhere in the table and then press the **F9** key. You will get a dialog box that asks whether you want to update only the page numbers or the entire table. If you update the entire table, you will lose any manual revisions to the table that you have made, as described in the previous section, so choose this option if you have not added any new headings to the dissertation. If you update only the page numbers, Word 2003 will retain the previous entries in the table of contents, including any manual changes, and will simply revise their page numbers. Click **OK** after making your choice.

8.3.6   *Update lists of equations, figures, and tables*

Similarly, you should make sure that your lists of equations, figures, tables, and the like have correct page numbers. To update a list, click once anywhere in the list and then press the **F9** key. You will get a dialog box that asks whether you want to update only the page numbers or the entire table. If you update the entire list, you will lose any manual revisions to entries in the list that you have made. If you update only the page numbers, Word 2003 will retain the previous entries in the list, including any manual changes, and will simply revise their page numbers. Click **OK** after making your choice.

8.4   Save the dissertation

After all these changes and updates, be sure to save the dissertation again. Click **File** and **Save**.

8.5   Printing the dissertation

To print the dissertation, click on **File** and **Print** to bring up the **Print** dialog box (Figure 8-12). From the **Name** drop-down menu, pick the printer that you wish to use. In the **Page range** section, identify what pages you want to print: **All**, for the entire document; **Current page**, for the page where your cursor now is; or **Pages,** if you want to specify certain pages. For this last option, you can use hyphens to designate a range (3–5) and commas to separate pages and/or ranges (1,3,5–7).

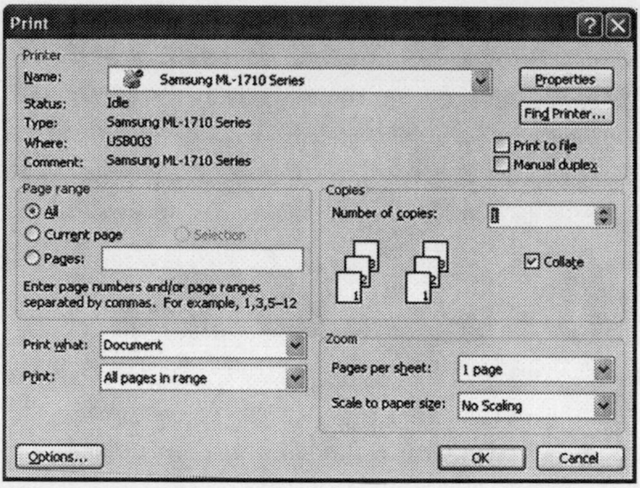

Figure 8-12

For a draft copy, you may want to try to save paper. One option is to print two pages side by side on a single sheet. To do this, pick **2 pages** from the **Pages per sheet** drop-down menu. (Obviously, for a formal printout of your dissertation, this should be set to **1 page**.)

Click on **OK** when you have set your printing options.

8.5.1   *Printing page numbers on landscape pages*

If you had to print one or more landscape orientation pages without page numbers (section 3.5), now is the time to add the page numbers. Determine the specific page numbers that need to be added. For each one, use your dissertation template to create a new, separate Word 2003 document (section 2.1). This document is to be completely blank except for the page number that you want applied to the landscape page. Set the page to that number by clicking on **Insert** and **Page Numbers** and then the **Format** button to get the **Page Number Format** dialog box. Set the **Start at** field to the page number that you want the landscape page to have. For example, Figure 8-13 shows how to set a page's number to 151. Now insert the landscape page into your printer's feed tray, and print the page by clicking on **File** and **Print** and then **OK**. The printer will print the portrait orientation page number on the paper that previously was printed in landscape orientation.

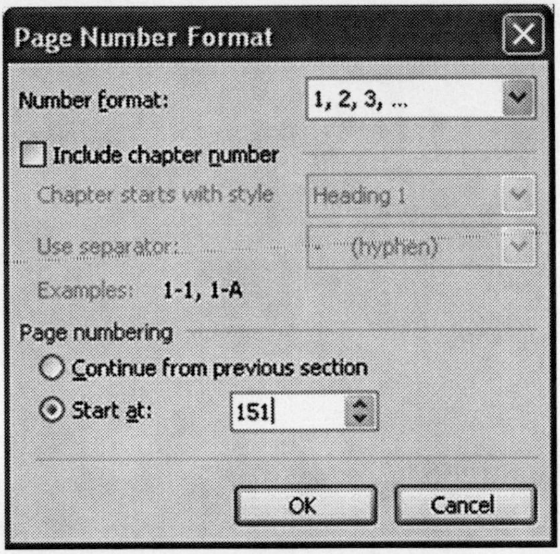

Figure 8-13

Note: Positioning the landscape page properly in the feed tray can be tricky, so you may want to practice once with a photocopy of your landscape page before you try the real thing. If you need a new copy of the landscape page, open your dissertation and click on **File** and **Print**. In the **Pages** field, list the page or pages that you need printed and click **OK**. Figure 8-14 shows how to print out page 151.

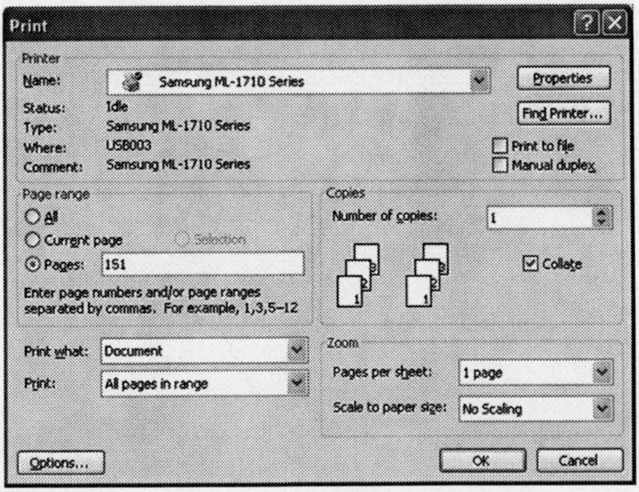

Figure 8-14

Chapter 9

A few words to the wise

You are investing hundreds, or even thousands, of hours in the preparation of your thesis or dissertation. Unfortunately, any number of technical problems can destroy that work—a lightning strike to the power line that supplies your computer, an attack by a virus that makes your hard disk unreadable, or even an editing error on your own part. As a result, you should consider some simple steps that can help prevent problems from happening and help you cope with them if they do crop up.

9.1   Antivirus software

Obtain, and use, antivirus software on the computer that you are using to write your dissertation. It can be a heartbreaking experience to discover that your computer—and perhaps your previous files as well—have been corrupted by a virus or worm. Many universities make antivirus software available to students at little or no cost, but even if your university doesn't, you should purchase it on your own.

And simply installing the software is not sufficient. Because new viruses and worms are constantly appearing, it is vital that you periodically update your computer's database of antivirus information. Follow the instructions in your antivirus program to do so, or preferably configure it to automatically update itself periodically.

9.2   Firewalls

It is likewise important to use a firewall to shield your computer from hacking attacks. If your computer is in a departmental office, it may well already have firewall protection, but if your computer is connected to the Internet from home, it may have no firewall protection. Recent versions of Microsoft Windows have basic firewalls that will provide a sufficient degree of protection—but you must first activate the firewall. Ask your university's IT help desk for help if necessary to get this important form of protection activated.

9.3   Windows updates

A third way to help make sure that your dissertation is not derailed by a hacker attack is to keep your computer's copy of Windows up to date. Microsoft periodically issues patches that are aimed at correcting weaknesses in Windows that can be exploited by hackers. By downloading and installing these patches, you can improve your computer's security. To check for patches for your machine, visit *http://windows update.microsoft.com*. Windows XP also offers a facility for automatically downloading updates; strongly consider using it.

9.4   Office updates

One more way to strengthen your computer is to download any patches for Word 2003 or Office 2003 (if you installed Word as part of Office). These patches include fixes for both bugs in the software and vulnerabilities that can be exploited by viruses and worms. Check *http://office.microsoft.com/officeupdate/* or click on **Help** and **Check for Updates**.

9.5   AutoRecover

Word 2003 can be configured to store information about open files on a regular basis. Word 2003 can use this information to try to restore the files if your computer crashes or if you suffer a power failure.

The default setting is to store the information every 10 minutes. You can set a different interval by clicking on **Tools** and then **Options** and then the **Save** tab (Figure 9-1). Be sure that the **Save AutoRecover info every** box is checked, and in the next box enter the interval, in minutes, for AutoRecover saves.

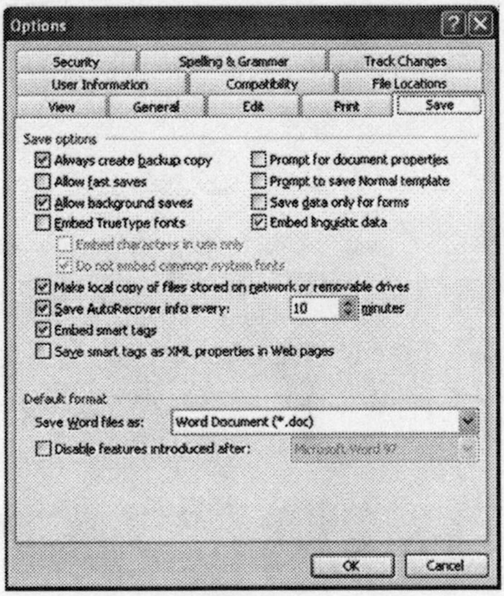

Figure 9-1

Note that AutoRecover is not a replacement for manually saving your files. Your own save may be more current than the AutoRecover save.

You also can change the location where AutoRecover files are saved. Click on **Tools** and then **Options** and then the **File Locations** tab (Figure 9-2). The entry for "AutoRecover files" will show the location where AutoRecover files are placed. To change this, highlight the AutoRecover entry and click on the **Modify** button (Figure 9-3). Navigate to the drive and folder where you want the AutoRecover files to go; you may want to consider saving them on your university's network file server, if possible. Click **OK** to return to the **File Locations** tab, and then **OK** again.

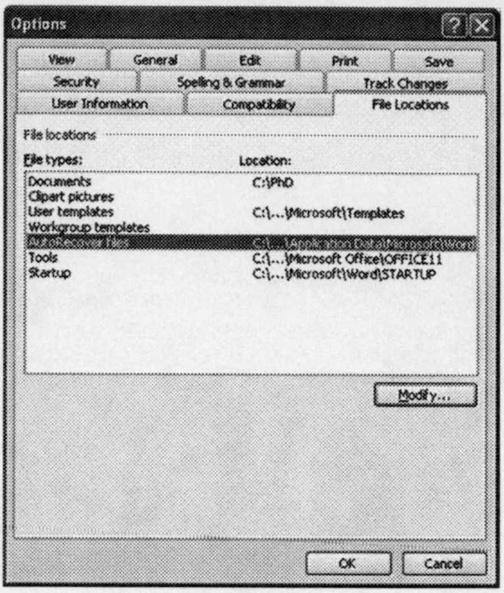

Figure 9-2

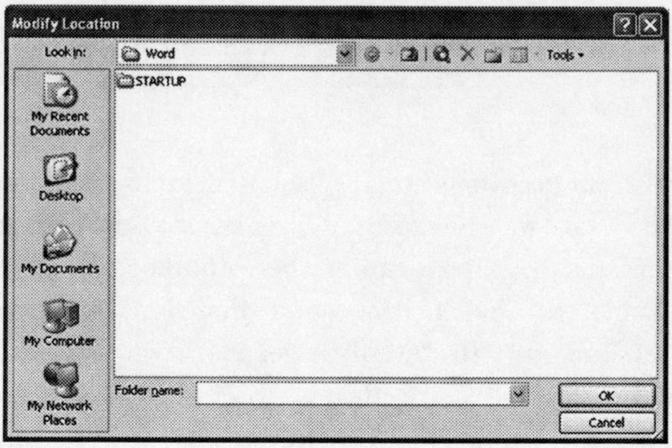

Figure 9-3

9.6   Automatic backups

You can program Word 2003 so that it saves the previous version of your file with a .bak extension whenever you save a new version of the file. This may be helpful if your file is accidentally corrupted—or if you simply want to see a previous version of what you had written.

To set this option, click on **Tools** and then **Options** and then the **Save** tab (Figure 9-1). Check the **Always create backup copy** box, and click **OK**.

9.7   Local copy

You can also instruct Word 2003 to save an extra copy of your files on your computer's own hard disk whenever you save to a network server or removable media like a Zip drive. This may not seem necessary if you are using your university's file server to store your dissertation files, since the university's server is probably well maintained and suffers few failures. But taking this step may give you some additional peace of mind.

To set the option, click on **Tools** and **Options** and then the **Save** tab. Check the box labeled **Make local copy of files stored on network or removable drives** (see Figure 9-1).

9.8   Back up frequently

If you store any dissertation-related files on your local computer, you should back up those files on a regular basis. Backups give you a fallback position if a file becomes corrupted by a software or hardware problem, and they also can be useful to consult if you change your mind about a new version of your writing.

Many universities provide students with a designated amount of file space on the university's computer system. This is often an ideal place for storing backup copies of your dissertation files. One aspect that makes it ideal is the fact that the network server is physically in a different location than your own computer, so if your computer is stolen or damaged in a fire, the backup copies on the server will not be damaged. Also, universities tend to back up their file servers with great regularity, so even if the file server itself becomes damaged, an earlier backup of your files from the previous day or week should be available. If your university does not provide file storage for students, you may want to investigate commercial file backup services, at least for the period during which you're writing your dissertation. For the importance of the dissertation in your academic career, spending $100 for a year of file storage probably would be a wise investment.

Windows XP includes software for backing up files that probably is compatible with your university's network; your university's IT support desk should be able to tell you how to use it or other software to schedule regular backups that can occur without any action on your part.

Character codes

Following is the table of codes for a variety of special symbols in Windows for the Times New Roman font (section 2.7). To enter a special symbol in this fashion, be sure the cursor is at the location in your file where you want to insert the special character. Check that the **Num Lock** light on your keyboard is on, which activates the numeric keyboard on the right-hand side of your keyboard. Then, while holding down the **ALT** key, use the numeric keyboard (not the number keys at the top of your keyboard) to type **0** followed by the three-number code selected from the table. For example, to enter the copyright symbol in this fashion, you would hold down the **ALT** key and type **0169** on the numeric keyboard.

Character code	Symbol
128	€
129	☐
130	‚
131	ƒ
132	„
133	…
134	†
135	‡

136	ˆ
137	‰
138	Š
139	‹
140	Æ
141	☐
142	Ž
143	☐
144	☐
145	'
146	'
147	"
148	"
149	•
150	–
151	—
152	-
153	™
154	š
155	›
156	æ
157	☐
158	ž
159	Ÿ
160	non-breaking space
161	¡
162	¢
163	£
164	¤
165	¥
166	¦
167	§
168	¨
169	©
170	ª
171	«

172	¬
173	-
174	®
175	—
176	°
177	±
178	²
179	³
180	´
181	µ
182	¶
183	·
184	¸
185	¹
186	º
187	»
188	¼
189	½
190	¾
191	¿
192	À
193	Á
194	Â
195	Ã
196	Ä
197	Å
198	Æ
199	Ç
200	È
201	É
202	Ê
203	Ë
204	Ì
205	Í
206	Î
207	Ï

208	Đ
209	Ñ
210	Ò
211	Ó
212	Ô
213	Õ
214	Ö
215	×
216	Ø
217	Ù
218	Ú
219	Û
220	Ü
221	Ý
222	Þ
223	ß
224	à
225	á
226	â
227	ã
228	ä
229	å
230	æ
231	ç
232	è
233	é
234	ê
235	ë
236	ì
237	í
238	î
239	ï
240	ð
241	ñ
242	ò
243	ó

244	ô
245	õ
246	ö
247	÷
248	ø
249	ù
250	ú
251	û
252	ü
253	?
254	?
255	ÿ

SUGGESTED READINGS

The following books may help you plan the style for your thesis or dissertation. As always, check with your graduate school and your adviser before deciding to follow the dictates of a particular style manual.

American Psychological Association. (2001). *Publication manual of the American Psychological Association* (5th ed.). Washington, DC: American Psychological Association.

CBE Style Manual Committee. (1994). *Scientific style and format: The CBE manual for authors, editors, and publishers* (6th ed.). Cambridge: Cambridge University Press.

The Chicago manual of style (15th ed.). (2003). Chicago: University of Chicago Press.

Gibaldi, J., & Modern Language Association of America. (2003). *MLA handbook for writers of research papers* (6th ed.). New York: Modern Language Association of America.

Nicol, A.A.M., Pexman, P. M., & American Psychological Association. (1999). *Presenting your findings: A practical guide for creating tables* (1st ed.). Washington, DC: American Psychological Association.

Turabian, K. L., Grossman, J., & Bennett, A. (1996). *A manual for writers of term papers, theses, and dissertations* (6th ed.). Chicago: University of Chicago Press.

INDEX

LaVergne, TN USA
05 January 2010
168858LV00005B/138/A